EXPECTATIONS
and
BURNOUT

Women Surviving the
Great Commission

EXPECTATIONS
and
BURNOUT

Women Surviving the Great Commission

Sue Eenigenburg and **Robynn Bliss**

WILLIAM CAREY
LIBRARY

Published by William Carey Library
1605 E. Elizabeth Street
Pasadena, CA 91104 | www.missionbooks.org

Beth Barron, copyeditor
Johanna Deming, editor
Jonathan Pon, graphic design

William Carey Library is a ministry of the U.S. Center for World Mission
Pasadena, CA | www.uscwm.org

Printed in the United States of America

16 15 14 13 12   7 6 5 4 3   BP1000

Library of Congress Cataloging-in-Publication Data

Eenigenburg, Susan E.
    Expectations and burnout : women surviving the great commission / Sue
    Eenigenburg, Robynn Blyss.
        p. cm.
    Includes bibliographical references.
    ISBN 978-0-87808-523-1
    1. Women in missionary work. 2. Burn out (Psychology)--Religious aspects--
Christianity. I. Blyss, Robynn. II. Title.
    BV2610.E36 2010
    248.8'43--dc22

                                    2010014203

DEDICATION

Above all, to our Savior, who accepts us as we are, shapes us as He wills, and restores us for His glory.

To our husbands, Don and Lowell, who inspire us by using their gifts while encouraging us to use ours.

To Sue's married four children and three adorable grandchildren— Stephen & Emily and their daughters Sophie and Stacy, Michael & Jayme and their daughter Alivia, Kristi & Alex, and Katie & Jeff

To Robynn's three children—Connor, Adelaide and Bronwynn— who bend our knees and delight our hearts.

To our parents, Buck & Nell Downey and Gary & Joan Allyn, who raised us well and love us still.

CONTENTS

FOREWORD

Three weeks after moving to Cairo, Sue sat me down and, with a serious expression on her face, stated, "I'm ready to go home." Since arriving, it seemed everything that could go wrong did go wrong. We were robbed, temperatures were soaring, everyone was sick. One morning she woke me up and asked me to go to the store. "We are out of diapers, toilet paper, tissues, paper towels. I have nothing to wipe what's spewing out of both ends of our kids." As I shuffled to the front door I noticed she was crying. Astutely I queried, "What's wrong?" She mumbled, "Today's your birthday and I didn't get you anything." The only response I could think of was, "If we make it through the day it will be a happy birthday."

Sitting in the living room soon after that, I was confronted with the option of throwing in the towel. Our prior two years studying language in a nearby country seemed manageable; our two month visit to our host city a year earlier was pleasant; but our reality at that moment seemed overwhelming. I looked around at all the recently-emptied trunks and proposed, "If you repack all the trunks, I'll go with you." She thought for a moment then countered, "Let's give it a few more days."

Life did not improve quickly, but we learned to cope. Sue is no self-acclaimed adventurer. She challenges herself to do one adventurous thing a year. Currently, she calculates that she's decades ahead of schedule! Despite her penchant for routine, God seems to have repeatedly forced her out of her comfort zone and helped her to thrive amazingly. How does she do it?

Let me take a little credit for at least adding to the pressure that brought Sue to the point of growth. I come from solid Dutch stock. Our twisted motto could be "Godliness is next to cleanliness!" We like neatness. We scrub roads! When Sue and I met, I thought it quaint that Sue would brag about her "hillbilly" roots. Once we got married it wasn't so amusing. Reality struck when the laundry pile overflowed prompting her to muse, "Somebody should do something about that. Oh, maybe that's me!" I like a house that's orderly, everything put away. Sue says her idea of cleaning is "sweeping the room with a glance." My expectations were high. Sue worked to live up to those expectations for a while, but eventually began to buckle.

I don't remember when it was, but it had something to do with Sue working through the book *Search for Significance*. It began to dawn on her that her value was not based on performing for the approval of others. Gradually, she unlocked the shackle of trying to meet my expressed and perceived demands. Her new question became, "How can I love others in the peculiar way God made me, rather than trying to conform to others' image of what I should be like?" I didn't like it at first. After all my way--the Dutch way--was the best, wasn't it? How was I going to control this wild woman if she no longer felt bound by my expectations?

Ultimately, I was humbled to learn that this new arrangement was much better. Sue's new freedom elevated her to another level. I began to like what God was doing to my woman as she submitted herself first to Him and launched out in the freedom of His grace. So we're different – what else is new? I like to get my work done and then play. She likes to intersperse play with her work. It's amazing what she can accomplish when she's having fun.

This book began as a thesis for graduate school. It contains research and theory. But it is much more than that. It's our life. It's an attack on the strongholds that bind women, forcing them to cower before the unrealistic expectations of others. My prayer is that as you allow the truths that unfold in this book to flood your soul, you will learn to live unleashed from the real and perceived demands of others. Dare we embrace the yoke of Jesus? Is it truly "easy"? Is his burden really "light"? There's only one way to find out.

– Don Eenigenburg

When I first left for the mission field, I was single—which made me target-number-one for matchmakers. As I was leaving for the Christar Hindu evangelism training program in Brooklyn, NY, I even got an aerogramme from my older sister, who was serving in Pakistan alongside Robynn's family. She wrote, "Would you like to meet a woman who wears a nose pin, knows how to make chappati, is great with children…?"

In my then thirty years of bachelorhood, I was always curious which bride people had in mind for me, but once I found out, I was then determined to avoid her at all costs. And so it was with Robynn, who was at the same training program directing the children's care. Others chimed in to match me with Robynn: veteran missionaries, fellow appointees, even the pastor of the host church. I was assisted in my avoidance of Robynn by the fact that she too was trying to match make me with one of her girlfriends. And yet, Robynn's charms worked on me sufficiently to make me ask a question I had never asked before: everyone speaking to me about Robynn—including my sister—I considered to be wise counselors in other areas of life; why shouldn't I listen to them in this area? Why shouldn't I listen for the voice of God in their voices? And so I prayed, "Lord, please show me what you see in Robynn." BAM—I fell in love and was filled with the Spirit in the same moment.

On the last evening of the program, I invited Robynn out for a cup of coffee. Loyal to the end, Robynn asked, "Can I bring my friend?" I replied, "No, just you and me." It was our only date. Three weeks later I left for my first term in South Asia. Robynn claims that I proposed to her in a letter that I wrote in Bangkok during a layover on that first trip to my host country. I didn't. Instead I was trying to convey to her the recognition that life on the mission field re-prioritizes *everything*, including the set of qualities that you admire in a potential spouse. Little did I know that I was inviting her into the expectations which fuel burnout.

I did do better when I actually did propose. Robynn came out to South Asia in the middle of my first year there. We met in the capital and had day-long conversations in the Rose Garden in Hauz Khas. We joined our team on a chaperoned vacation on the tropical beaches of a nearby city, where we could hold hands and have our first kiss. My intention was to let Robynn travel first to my adopted city before popping the question. The locale of my calling can be a difficult place to live. I thought it only fair to let Robynn see what she was getting herself into—what to expect, if you will.

However, by the time we passed through the capital awaiting our train to go see this city, in the next couple days, I was of a different mind. I felt I needed to show Robynn my conviction that marriage (as a calling) is more important than ministry. Or that ministry grows out of marriage. If she couldn't "make it" in this part of the world, my commitment to her would still strongly lead us to the next place the Lord had in mind for us as one. Robynn was more important than a location for ministry. I would invest my future in her, not it. And so, on the lawn of the Imperial Hotel, in the remaining aura of the British Raj over afternoon tea and caramel custard, I asked her, "Will you marry me?"

The writer of a foreword is something of a matchmaker. The nature of the stories of expectation and burn-out that Robynn shares in this book will presume a degree of relationship between you the reader and Robynn and Sue, the authors. A good portion of the pain in these stories, as in all our stories, is a desire to be loved. And sure enough, often in our sixteen years of marriage, I've wished people would see the things that I see in Robynn and love her as much as I do. But any sort of storytelling, whether over a cup of coffee or as words on a printed page, presumes risk. Thinking biblically, it presumes a trust in Christ that He will accomplish His goodwill in speaker and listener both. The best I can do as a matchmaker is to share my own testimony. Begin this book with a prayer: "Lord, open my eyes to what You want me to see in the lives and writing of Robynn and Sue." Believe me, it's a prayer that will enrich your life.

I am the only one in the world who can attest to Robynn's honesty in this book—not even Sue can give you that assurance. While wanting to respect that mysterious and private place in Robynn's soul and in her womanly heart, nonetheless these stories are as much mine as hers. We lived them out together. I can assure you that she has spoken with honesty, except in her failure to make public my many sins and shortcomings as her husband during these times. That's just the mark of the grace that I have known from her all along.

There were times during some of the many trials that Robynn hasn't written about that we'd turn to each other with a laugh and say, "Well, at least this will make a great prayer letter." We never lacked for material. But that probably says more about God than it does about our city. He values faith and never tires at building it in us. He is the Master Discipler and the whole world is His classroom.

Robynn and Sue's book may be the one you are reading, but your own experience as a woman on the mission field—your own experience of expectation and burn-out—is the book that God is writing. While I commend you to Robynn and Sue's authorship, I more wholeheartedly commend you to God's. We often think of the "great cloud of witnesses" as a body of exceptional believers watching over us. With our own perceptions of such women as Lillias Trotter, Elisabeth Elliot, or Amy Carmichael, there can be a whole new set of self-imposed expectations that fatigue us. And yet, the "great cloud of witnesses" can also be understood as a group for which the Lord is fitting us for membership. You will one day join your story with theirs, testifying not to the perfection of missionary women, but to the goodness of God experienced in your endurance.

– Lowell Bliss

ACKNOWLEDGMENTS

There are many people along the way that should certainly be thanked—and we're not simply referring to the writing process. There have been people that have brought a word of encouragement on a dark day, people that exhorted, loved on, or ministered to us in our moments of brokenness and seasons of despair. How can we ever begin to tell each of you how grateful we are to God for the ways you kept us going? God used you to preserve our sanity when it seemed like we might be losing it. He used you to keep us from completely going over the edge! Thank you.

There are some specific people we'd like to thank.

We are thankful to each of the 323 women who saw the importance of this topic and invested their time to complete the survey we sent out.

We are thankful for Dr. Delray Schultz who helped analyze all of the data from those surveys.

Beth Barron, our editor, spent more hours than we can imagine going over our writing to correct, edit and improve. Bev Guy was our extremely capable and helpful proof reader. Sue's daughter Kristi helped with proofreading as well.

Scott and Julie Coonrod opened their home to Sue for a week and gave their dining room table as our office where we worked on this book.

Thank you to the co-workers that God surrounded us with in our areas of service. You were our family. You were our community. We grew to love you all deeply. Thank you.

Thanks to Christar who over the years has empowered us to use our spiritual gifts in accordance with our calling. Most recently, of course, this has meant giving us the freedom to write. Thank you.

We are deeply thankful to churches and people who pray, give and support us in our ministries. God has used you to enrich our lives and enable us to serve for His glory among the nations.

Robynn wants to say ...

I would like Ellen & Neepa to know how grateful I am for the countless, year-in-year-out ways Jesus blessed me through you both.

Thanks to Mom and Auntie Carol and the countless adopted "aunties" who showed me how to grow up and how to be a missionary woman. You taught me flexibility and creativity. You showed me what faith and optimism look like in a spiritually-bleak environment. You gave me a sense of humor and taught me how to make almost anything out of almost nothing. I learned a great deal from you and I'm grateful.

Thanks also to the Pastors at Faith Evangelical Free Church in Manhattan, Kansas (Steve, Brian, Russ, Chris and Micah) who extended much grace and gave me the freedom to write on top of the job you paid me to do! Thanks to Janelle who filled in the gaps and made it look like I always got my work done! Thanks to our small group (the Renbergs & the Griegers) and the mission's prayer breakfast crew and others who prayed this book to completion.

Thank you to Lowell who knew when to put the red pen away and when to just hold me and cry with me. Thanks to Connor, Adelaide and Bronwynn for being patient during this time... even though Auntie Sue didn't quite make me famous.

Sue closes with ...

I appreciate Don who encouraged me to pursue writing and enabled me to invest time into communicating things dear to my heart. He loved and comforted me when I didn't meet expectations and also cheered me when I surprised myself and exceeded some.

My heartfelt thanks to Chapel Hill Church where I grew up knowing I was loved, learning the Word of God, and where my desire to serve God was fanned and given wings.

My past teammates, co-workers in the office, and present teammates have enriched my life and extended grace to me.

Sincere thanks to Heidi, Jamie, MaryAnn, Nan and Rosie who specifically prayed for me and encouraged me as I was writing.

I wouldn't be here to write if my sister hadn't saved me from drowning. Thank you, Debbie, for rescuing me.

In closing, Robynn and I recognize that we are both surrounded by God's goodness and we are very grateful!

CONNECT

We would welcome the opportunity to interact with you about what we've written.

You can contact Robynn through her website: www.edenvigil.org. She also invites you to learn more about her and Lowell's newest venture in environmental missions there.

You can catch up with Sue and read about some of her adventures in ministry and what she's learning through her blog: http://screamsinthedesert.wordpress.com/. She would love to hear from you. Post a comment either about the book or the most recent blog entry.

INTRODUCTION

We are all trying to do what God has asked us to do, but certainly there are some of us who try too hard to keep up with the image of what we feel a missionary should be like. – Marjory Foyle

In over 20 years of missionary experience I have seen many missionaries come and go. I have seen perseverance, vacillation, discouragement, encouragement, success and failure. I've had sweet times of fellowship on teams. I've experienced some heartbreaking team meetings that seemed so opposite of what I would have expected before arriving on the field. My children have had loving missionary "aunts and uncles" and we have some very close friends because we weathered missionary life together. There have been those who have had many years of ministry and others who have either experienced burnout or left prematurely. It is true that God does lead people away from missions to other ministries, but I think it is safe to say that sometimes people may give up too soon or work in such a way that burnout causes them to leave a long-term missions career.

I left for my first term with high expectations of all that I would accomplish. It didn't take long to realize that God needed to do more in me before He could accomplish what He wanted to do through me. This was not exactly what I had planned. I remember the exhaustion, feeling tempted to give up and seeking encouragement from God and others. How thankful I am for those who have prayed for us and partnered with us in ministry.

After coming back to the states to work in the U.S. office, I decided to further my education at the same time. To complete graduate school in 2008, I needed to come up with a research project. I knew I wanted to study about missionaries and burnout. Through a painful process of narrowing down my topic (Dr.

Elaine Huber knows what I am talking about!), I came up with researching the correlation between expectations and burnout. It was a fascinating project and one that was especially meaningful to me since I had held unrealistic expectations of myself and others.

While reading the research of others, I decided to do my own survey and sent it to several mission agencies. I am deeply grateful for their help in sending it to their missionary women who had at least four years of missionary experience. I received 323 completed surveys. I am thankful to each of these 323 women who saw the importance of this topic and invested their time to fill out the survey. In the responses, I saw that many women were like me–dealing with expectations, both real and perceived, and sometimes feeling close to burnout. I am thankful for Dr. Delray Schultz who helped analyze all the data from those surveys.

Not wanting only statistics and dry research in a book, I also wanted to add a personal touch. I asked my friend Robynn Bliss to share her story with you. I have long admired this younger woman with a passion for God and a zeal for the lost. Whenever I am around her, she inspires me to love God more and impassions my desire to reach the lost. She experienced burnout and God has brought her through it. Though it wasn't easy for her to write about it, she has because of her love for God and others.

After months of working separately we were ready to meet face to face. We had our editor's helpful comments in front of us (thank you, Beth Barron!). As we sat together at Scott and Julie Coonrod's dining room table looking out at the beautiful fall colors of the Kansas landscape, we worked on this book together. We shared our stories and our lives, we wrote and rewrote and we prayed that God would use this book to enlarge His kingdom around the world.

Interspersed throughout this book you will find Robynn's story. You will also read data, quotes and illustrations taken directly from the surveys that were sent to missionary women around the world. I will share a part of my story as well. Robynn and I pray that God will use this book to help missionary women, mission agencies, sending churches and host cultures to better understand what the real and perceived expectations are for us as missionary women and what our expectations are of them. There are some expectations that need to be intentionally abandoned. Others need to be more aligned with reality. Still others need to be fanned and encouraged. May God be at work as we work through these expectations and focus on all He will do to help us burn brightly, rather than burnout, for Him and His glory among the nations.

– Sue

One year, Daphne, a woman the age of my mother came to visit. She had heard all manner of things about our city. She had heard about the poverty, the dead being cremated at the water's edge, dead bodies floating down the river, misshapen beggar children roaming the streets, masses and millions swarming the markets. No doubt she had also heard wild stories of spiritual warfare in our town: demons visible, oppression felt, dramatic prayers with equally dramatic results! She had heard it all and she had unknowingly formed expectations about how the city would be, what she would see, how she would respond.

Daphne's expectations colored her experience. She looked for things she didn't necessarily see, but she almost saw them from looking so hard! I think she was a little sad that she didn't see a dead body bouncing on the top of the river. I think she was a little put out that no obvious dark spiritual forces engaged her. She didn't see any demons. How disappointing! Her imagination kicked in, though, and filled in some of the gaps. She had expectations and they had to be realized! Daphne expected hard things in our city and she left thinking it was hard because admitting anything

3

else would have meant grave disappointment. It also would have meant she had been wrong.

In my own experience I've seen how my thinking of something ahead of time, my dreaming and praying, my planning and imagining have all come to affect the outcomes of my life's stories. I've set myself up for disappointment many times over the years. I've thought I knew what was coming. I knew how God would act, how He would lead me, how He would answer. But it hasn't gone that way. When that happens what should be a comforting theological truth that God is sovereign becomes an annoyance and a disconcerting reality that even God is not as I expected Him to be.

One night while Daphne was staying with us, we had friends over for dinner. After a delicious chicken curry we settled in to watch a movie on our newly acquired little black and white television. Daphne said she'd just go to bed. A little while later she called for me from her room. I pushed my eight-and-a-half-months-pregnant body to the edge of my chair and labored to get up. I wobbled along to her room trying to be quick so as not to miss much of the movie.

The lights were out in the guest room and Daphne was in her bed under the mosquito net. I asked what she needed and she said there was a mosquito in her net. I suggested she kill it. She said she couldn't find it and it was really bothering her. I turned on the light and together we searched for the pesky mosquito. I couldn't see it either. We looked and we looked. The soundtrack played on in the background, reminding me I was missing the climax of the film. Finally out of exasperation, selfishness and frustration, I slapped my hands together feigning a death in the mosquito world. "There!" I said …

Daphne thanked me and I turned off the light and went back to my movie. Daphne fell asleep ... Once again her expectations proved wrong. She thought I was a selfless, kindly friend honestly helping her kill a tiny foe. Unfortunately and to my shame, she was wrong.

— Robynn

ONE

THE EXPLORATION BEGINS, A STUDY OF EXPECTATIONS AND BURNOUT

It seems apparent from the literature reviewed that the height of our expectations is an important factor in burnout.—W.E. Dyment

I could not wait to arrive overseas. I had been to Bible college and my husband had graduated from seminary. Considered spiritually mature for a young woman, I led women's Bible studies. I had a passion for least-reached peoples and had attended our mission's New Personnel Orientation as well as a language learning program. Books on Islam and training in evangelism and discipleship completed my training. After having my shots, and getting a passport and visa, I was ready. We packed our bags and, though it was hard, said goodbye to family.

Following through with God's call on my life to serve Him in another culture, I envisioned learning the language quickly, leading many nationals to the Lord, planting a church and being successful in ministry. I knew about culture shock, had read books about it and felt prepared for our move overseas. Our children would adapt well, I had heard, as long as we did, so I had no worries about that. Move over Elizabeth Elliot, I was on my way!

Nothing could have prepared me for the shock of arriving in the middle of the night to an unwelcoming airport with unsmiling, machine-gun-toting soldiers. My husband, children and I were picked up and dropped off at a house where no one spoke English. We didn't know where we were or who we were staying with. We arrived and saw a group of men leave the bedroom into which our family of five was ushered. There had been no time to change the sheets, but we were so tired we didn't care (well, not much).

Our hosts served us a light dinner. Were we supposed to drink the water? Did we pay for this? How much should we eat? The next morning I awoke to the call to prayer and we began our search for a place to live before language school started in a few days. There was so much to do and so little we knew. How thankful I am to those who came alongside and helped us. We started language school and I learned how to ask my first question in a new language, "Where is the bag?"

After several months of studying, mothering, cooking, cleaning, shopping and trying to survive I concluded that I must have misunderstood God. Where was the fruit of my ministry? I couldn't lead anyone to Christ; I was still trying to find out where the bag was! I was tired, disillusioned and felt like quitting. This missionary life was not what I had expected. I had envisioned something so totally different.

My husband seemed to be catching on more quickly, more able to study and more certain of his role. I felt like I was floundering and wondered if I was the only one who felt unable to be who I wanted to be or to do all I wanted to do. I was not meeting my own expectations. I felt unable to keep up with all I felt I was supposed to be able to accomplish.

Of course now, years later, I know that I am not the only one who experienced this gap between what my expectations were and what my reality actually was. Through talking with other missionary women and my own observations, I have realized that it is quite common. I also was hearing more about burnout among missionaries and I began to wonder if there was any correlation between these high expectations and burnout among missionary women. In order to finish graduate school I did some research into this possible relationship between expectations and burnout and was intrigued. I wanted to discover more about expectations to see if there was a link between these normally unrealistic expectations and the rise of burnout I was observing as I interacted with missionary women.

I began to read and study what experts had discovered. I learned that though some psychological research has been done on women missionaries, most of it is gender neutral. In the past most research has been done by men writing about missionaries and issues relevant to missions. Much has been written from a man's perspective, but it was more difficult to find much information specific to women, even though most mission agencies have more women as members than men.

Women and men are both critical in church planting, yet only recently has much been written by and about women missionaries and their work. Although many issues, like culture stress and church-planting strategies, are as relevant to men as women in missions, there are issues such as balancing roles, finding a niche in ministry and dealing with sexual harassment that may be more relevant for women. Also, women experience culture stress differently from men and tend to experience more stress than men. Married women often have more time management issues as they balance their ministry in the home with ministry outside of the home. Single women have a particular set of issues they must face as well as they deal with constant assumptions and questions as to why they are single as well as having to do so many things on their own.

It has been exciting since the late '90s to see more women writing books and articles as well as networking at conferences to share these resources specifically for and about women missionaries. Although several research studies have laid a good foundation on the roles and needs of women missionaries, more research needs to be done to better understand and help missionary women.

It is painful to me to see missionaries leave ministry due to preventable causes. The rate of attrition and burnout for missionaries is alarming and needs to be addressed more thoughtfully. I am acquainted with one experienced missionary who is of the opinion that the younger generation of western missionaries is "softer" than those who are older. She thinks that they are not used to suffering or working hard, whereas older missionaries were used to a harder lifestyle with fewer luxuries. Agreeing that there are some differences between the work force today as opposed to the past, Taylor (1997) writes:

> Some North Americans, particularly, have come to expect that any venture they pursue will have a larger number of "givens" than past generations of missionaries had. This checklist includes things such as security, health plans, pension plans, retirement plans, educational needs of children, opportunities for continuing personal growth and development, leisure and recreational aspects, and unspoken guarantees regarding financial, physical and emotional security. (p. 243)

Of course, it could also be argued that the younger generation of missionaries has a stronger desire for deep and lasting relationships than older missionaries had. However, one thing that has not changed from one generation to the next is that most missionaries go into full-time ministry to serve God and see the world change through Jesus Christ for His glory.

Many mission leaders and caregivers have observed that most people going overseas have very high expectations of what can be accomplished. When talking with new missionaries, these leaders hear their high expectations for themselves, their mission agency, their co-workers, nationals, their sending church and God. Missionaries on the field are seeing more burnout as well. One missionary woman wrote on her survey, "I've seen a lot more burned out people— even first termers. Something is very wrong." New missionaries are passionate to change the world and ready to see God use them to do it. However, the harsh reality is that devotion and zeal appear to be no safeguard against burnout, and, in fact, may contribute to it.

Believing there is some correlation between expectations and burnout, missionary women can be better prepared for service by being made aware of the need to clarify their expectations. I don't remember anyone taking me aside and saying, "Sue, it is great you want to save the world, but let me tell you a little bit more about some of the challenges you will face as a woman in missions. Keep your excitement and faith in God who is working in and through you, but remember it is more about Him than you."

I honestly find it hard to discern to what degree my expectations were based on me and my passion to serve God my way and how much they were based on honoring God and wanting to follow His plan. While I would not suggest to a missionary to not expect anything, I do want missionary women to go into missions with their eyes open to what their expectations are of themselves and God, as well as what God might want to do in and through them. He is the God who does the impossible and we trust Him in everything. However, we can't make our expectations of who we should be or all we should do as missionaries the basis of our identity. One missionary woman who responded to the survey wrote what surprised her is how some missionaries feel about being missionaries and this passion to serve God:

> [I'm surprised] how psychologically wedded some people are
> to being missionaries. I've had people tell me, "if I weren't
> a missionary, I'd be nobody"—very scary and unhealthy

thinking. Additionally, how many missionaries' formal doctrine is salvation by grace, and lifestyle is salvation by works? Also… it's easy to preach grace and not give grace to each other.

We can follow William Carey's example to "attempt great things for God, expect great things from God." However, we also need to keep in mind that he tempered enthusiasm about what God would do with the reality of his situation. Beck (1992) described Carey's change in perspective: "The lack of India's receptivity to the gospel challenged Carey's evangelistic zeal. Carey's initial enthusiasm slowly gave way to a more realistic view regarding the responsiveness of the Indian subcontinent to Christianity" (p. 167). With all that William Carey accomplished, if he had to realign his enthusiastic expectations with reality, I think most missionaries today will have to do the same!

Also, mission agencies need to learn how to better prepare future missionary women to discover and evaluate their expectations of themselves, their teams, their mission agency and others. It will be important for both the organization and the missionary to differentiate between real expectations, what is in our ministry plans and communicated to us, and perceived ones, vague impressions of what we should be like or should be doing. Understanding the role of expectations in burnout has the potential to produce more effective training by mission agencies and healthier missionaries with longer careers of effective service.

It has been said that if the married missionary woman is dissatisfied or unhappy, the couple will leave the field (Chester, 1983), so caring well for missionary women is essential. Single women who feel uncared for or underutilized may not continue on in missions when other opportunities come their way. Though resources are examined that refer to others in ministry and burnout among other professions, my goal is to see how that information might relate to missionary women. The insights generated by the research for this book may not only help women missionaries, but also help couples as well to enjoy long-term missionary service and reach their full ministry potential.

There are some problems to consider when researching missionaries. Because of the hesitancy of some missionaries to admit to anger or burnout, they may deny having burned out and come up with more acceptable reasons for leaving their area of ministry. For some missionaries, to admit to burnout or anything else that may seem negative is to feel like a failure and risk being perceived as unspiritual. Vander Pol (1994) points to this hesitancy of missionaries when she states, "Most of the missionaries on the field reported to the interviewer that they felt pressure to behave in certain ways and felt that the expression of anger was inappropriate" (p. 34). I certainly remember wondering how much to share with our team in our first term. What would they think of me if I shared my struggles with them? Due to the missionaries' possible hesitancy to admit to negatively perceived emotions as well as burnout, the data elicited in this research may be understating unmet expectations and the rate of burnout. If we knew more accurately all of the facts and personal stories, I think we would be taken aback at how much expectations and burnout affect missionary women.

Addressing expectations and preventing burnout is crucial. Jesus gave the Great Commission to his followers to go into the entire world and preach the gospel. When missionary women burn out and leave their field of service, that hinders the opportunity of people, most of them women, in that community to hear about the Lover of their souls. May God use this research to help missionary women, mission agencies and sending centers become more aware of expectations and the role they play in burnout. As a result, by God's grace, missionary women will be better equipped and able to have long, effective careers in missions. Through this research, mission agencies also can learn how to help prepare missionary women to identify and deal with expectations to avoid burnout. Churches may also discover how they can better understand and support the missionaries they send as well as the role they play in determining expectations.

Everyone has expectations. Dyment (1989) reports that a person's expectations are influenced by significant others around her and that these expectations can be taken as her own or discarded as she forms her own identity. He goes on to say that when we have gone though this process, we form the "ego ideal" which is the combination of our highest expectations and beliefs about what we can accomplish and who we are. This then becomes our judge, our standard, when we are evaluating our own performances. We may try very hard to consistently live up to these highest ideals.

Missionaries are no exception to this. We have expectations of all we should accomplish based on things we've seen, heard and experienced. We look at ourselves and what we think we can or should accomplish. We see who we want to be and what we want to do and seek to live that out, which is good. However, if what we do becomes the determining factor on which we base our worth or significance, we may be in serious trouble. We have expectations, whether known or subliminal, about what life and ministry will be like as missionaries.

There are also expectations of missionaries by others. Everyone has a mental image of what a missionary should be like, from how they might look to how they should act. People expect missionaries to be good evangelists, rather poor, pious and actively doing good and caring for others overseas. Married missionary women should be a mostly perfect godly wife, mother and missionary. It is assumed this comes quite naturally because of their calling. When asked on the survey how they developed their view of what missionary women were like, women missionaries gave some good insight into the process:

◠ We always hear about the positives and the good stuff that is happening, but rarely do we hear about their struggles, frustrations, how much time they spend just living. It always sounds like they spend 100 percent of their time engaging nationals, are best friends with them. We never hear about the clothesline that broke with all of the wet clothes on it ... I think we do a disservice when we only tell the positives. I'm not saying we need to just complain and gripe, but a healthy dose of reality gives a much more accurate picture of our lives. It was a surprise to me to find that I couldn't spend all day one on one with women in discipleship and witnessing because that is what we hear about when we hear mission stories.

◠ [I saw them as] super Christians who really had it all together spiritually. I think that the churches that I grew up in sort of 'idolized' missionaries. They wanted us as kids to look up to missionaries and think of missions as a high calling, which was great; but we didn't get enough sense of missionaries as being real people who have weaknesses, who fail, who make mistakes, who sin and who have tempers.

◠ My view was that they were one step below the 12 apostles. I developed this image from leaders at church that taught us about missions, how the pastor introduced missionaries when they would come and speak and from reading about missionaries.

When I became a missionary I expected a lot of myself based on the "ego ideal." Added to that were the expectations I thought others had of missionaries, based on what I had seen, heard and read. Was I naïve to think I would become a bold evangelist, perfect wife, mother and church planter, like Billy Graham, Betty

Crocker and James Dobson all rolled into one when I became a missionary? Yes, I was naïve. However, these were some of my expectations of myself. When these two sets of expectations, who we think we should be and who we think others think we should be as missionaries, converge in the midst of a stressful new term, we might be tempted to deny the seriousness of our situation because we are supposed to be spiritual people above such things. We might also seek to escape a harsh reality by leaving emotionally, mentally and/or physically from a stressful situation.

By trying to keep up the image of a good missionary (Chester, 1983), missionaries may admit to burnout too late to get the help they need to stay in their chosen profession. This late admission might not be intentional; often missionaries can be unaware of the amount of stress they are under (Chester, 1983). It was only after leaving our first field of service that I was able to recognize the pressure under which I had been living: not knowing if our visas would be granted; wondering if the police would come to our door; dealing with a struggling small church plant; learning of an informant in our midst; helping others leave the country quickly; the constant stress of being a mother of four small children. At the time, living with a huge amount of stress had begun to feel normal. Though there is stress throughout a missionary's career, Koteskey (n.d.) points out, as do others, that the first term is especially tenuous:

> The time of greatest risk for burnout in any people-helping occupation is the first five years on the job. That is exactly the time frame of the first term and language school in most agencies. This new worker is filled with idealism and high expectations. When reality begins to set in, the first-term cross-cultural worker begins to burnout (para 12).

Vander Pol (1994) agrees with Koteskey (n.d.) about the susceptibility of first-term workers and shares research done by

Lindquist (1982), who reported that up to 50 percent of first-term missionaries return early or do not return after their first term. The first term is usually very difficult for missionaries. I know I would not want to go through my first term again! Many are seeking to live up to what they think missionaries should be like. Because of this pressure to perform, it seems some missionaries resist exposing their weaknesses or sharing struggles and, therefore, do not complain until they are already well down the path toward burnout. Chester (1983) asserts that missionaries feel pressure to portray that they are unaffected by difficulty to keep up the image of "Super Saint." Because they do not see stress evident in their co-workers, they do not want to let on that they are feeling stress. The results of Chester's (1983) research prove that though missionaries may feel under stress, they do not acknowledge it, realize its severity or show it:

> The missionaries were asked if they felt that missionary life was stressful. Thirty percent of the husbands (24 percent of the wives) reported that they felt it was very stressful. When asked if they felt that they "personally" were under more stress as a missionary, 59 percent of the husbands (62 percent of the wives) reported: "yes ..." (p. 31)

Due to this pressure for missionaries to appear close to perfect and reluctance to be open to sharing struggles, missionaries can hide many of the symptoms of burnout until it is impossible to do so any longer due to its severity. Two missionary women were surprised at how little people on their teams shared about struggles:

> I was really surprised at how guarded so many people were about struggles. And I don't even mean the deepest, darkest kind you only share with select close friends. I

17

mean things like, 'I'm struggling with culture shock' or 'Some days I really miss home' or 'Some days I really struggle to love the people here.' I would mention something like this as a request and people would look at me like I was really unspiritual or something for struggling with those things. I don't recall teammates offering to pray for me when I shared things like that. It was almost as if those concerns weren't spiritual enough to even pray about. I offered to pray for a teammate's sick child and they said, 'Don't worry about it. It's not a big deal.'

For the longest time I thought I was the only one who struggled with anything—and I felt really lonely because of that. Then I began to figure out that everyone else struggled too, but they put on the 'happy worker' face— maybe out of fear or being burned in the past or maybe out of the misguided notions that workers are supposed to be super-Christians or something. It has been good to find friends over the years (some in our organization and others in different organizations) who have been real with me. We have been able to share joys and struggles and encourage and pray for each other.

The source of this pressure to behave in certain ways must be examined. Taylor (1997) and Jones (1995) mention some of these sources: missionary self-expectations, family members, supporters, sending churches, mission home leadership, receiving church, other missionaries and professional peers. One not mentioned is media and how it influences expectations. One missionary woman vividly describes her own battle with expectations she had of herself as a result of reading missionary biographies:

18

It was nothing like what I expected and yet I didn't really know what to expect. I had read countless missionary biographies and I guess I expected my life to be like the stories I read. It was shocking to find out how difficult it was to not be able to communicate, to not recognize labels of food packages; it was devastating to leave crying children with baby sitters every morning. It was impossible to measure up to everything I thought I should do, or what I thought others thought I should do. I expected to be Wonder Woman, and when I wasn't, it was hard to accept.

We will explore six sources of expectations in this book:

1. **Self:** feeling acute failure as we fall short of our ideal version of a missionary.

2. **Sending church:** wondering if we let our supporters down by not having as many tangible results as we would like and they might expect.

3. **Mission agency:** appreciating the training, but not remembering it or feeling let down by how different everything is in our roles as women in cross-cultural ministry.

4. **Fellow missionaries:** looking forward to having best friends on our teams and feeling disillusioned with relationships.

5. **National friends and host culture:** expecting that we will love everyone we meet and letting our misunderstanding of a new culture color our view of people.

6. **God:** trying to understand our disappointment with God and talk about it when we are not supposed to feel disappointment with Him, but know we should trust Him no matter what.

Many of these expectations are experienced by both men and women; however, those more relevant to women will be more specifically addressed.

Before examining these major sources of expectations and perceived expectations, let me introduce you to my friend Robynn. I've invited her to share her story with you. She, her husband and family served in South Asia for around 14 years. She does a good job of putting flesh to the research so we can learn from her experience with expectations and burnout. Robynn will share her story, not only in the next chapter and the last one, but through several illustrations throughout the book.

Survival Tip #1
Remember you are
called, chosen, and clay

No matter where you are in your missionary career: whether you've just finished your application process, you've just joined your mission agency with joy and passion, or whether you've just completed your third term on the field. Maybe you've experienced some of what has been described in chapter one eating at the edges of your soul. Or possibly you've only just now realized that your reality is not matching how you thought things would be. No matter where you are at, reading through chapter one may have left you disheartened, deflated, and disappointed. I (Robynn) want to reassure you: there is hope!

At this point it might be good to remember a few things.

Remember that it was God who called you. He is in charge. He invited us to be a part of His Great Commission. He specifically spoke into your soul and called you out to be a part of this amazing worldwide thing that He is about! He chose you! Take a moment even now to pour yourself a cup of hot tea and rehearse the story of your specific calling.

Remember that God has used women in powerful ways in this Reconciliation Enterprise. Ever since Jesus stood in front of the twelve disciples and the crowd that had assembled with them and declared that we are to "go into all the world, and preach the gospel," women have been involved and to great effect! Remember the stories you've heard of women in missions. Remember the women missionaries you've met. Reread if you need to the *Guardians of the Great Commission* by Ruth Tucker. We are children of the Most High God and He loves us and uses us. We become Jesus to speak truth to the modern day women at the well. He uses us to point out their thirst. He uses us to pour out the Living Water.

Remember your personal value to your Heavenly Father. If you left your missionary journey right now, if you threw in the towel, if you checked out, hung up your apron and walked away—He would embrace you and love you. He would gather you up and wipe the tears from your face. He would whisper reassurances to your soul. He would say it doesn't matter. He loves you deeply and that love is not connected to what you do. It's who you are. You are His precious little girl, His beloved child. He is so completely committed to you—just because He is! He loves you.

Remember also that you are clay. That doesn't surprise God! When he chose you before the beginning of time to be His daughter, when he later called you to this Great Commission adventure, He knew you were clay! He is the potter; He molded you and formed you. And in the breaking, chipping, and cracking that will surely happen, if it hasn't already, His glory is revealed. Remember that "we have this treasure in jars of clay to show that this all-surpassing power is from God and not from us." (2 Corinthians 4:7, NIV) Being clay forces us to depend on God. We can't do it without him. If we could do it on our own, the glory wouldn't go to Him and to Him alone.

These are the things to remember. There is hope. God is in this with us. He loves us. He made us. And even more comforting is that He doesn't need to be reminded of all these things. He knows.

TWO

ROBYNN, A SURVIVOR'S STORY

No matter how thoroughly missionaries are prepared for going to their field of service, the reality is often far from their expectations.
– William D. Taylor

I remember the day we couldn't get out of bed. Actually we did get out of bed. I made the coffee and breakfast, packed up the kids' lunchboxes, got all three of them dressed in their white school uniforms, made sure their water bottles were full and waved them off. Lowell walked them to the gate to catch the auto rickshaw that would take them to school. And then we both went back to bed.

I think we must have gotten up for some lunch. There were a few knocks on the door, a few things to attend to. The kids eventually returned from school. They were washed, and homeworked and snacked and placed in front of a movie. Lowell and I went back to bed.

Supper was simple and easy. Lowell managed the energy to wrestle some with Connor and to read the required bedtime story to the girls. I cleaned up the kitchen, fed the dog and the cat. After the three children were in their beds, mosquito nets in place, ceiling fans on, Lowell and I went back to bed.

We were so tired. An accumulation of assorted circumstances had left us wrung out, weary and worn down. We pushed through that month and the next; various outreaches, an emergency appendectomy, a disgruntled teammate in another city demanding attention, a conference to lead. Life kept beating us down relentlessly. Maybe it was time to say it; maybe it was time to admit we were *burnt out*.

Certain words are best never said. We are firmly loyal to our marriage vows. We don't use the word *divorce*, not even lightly, not even in jest. It's a sacred thing, marriage. The word *divorce* erodes that. It also gives the imagination something to toy with, a place to end up when the love is stretched thin, when hurts don't heal quite so quickly, when the heart is bruised. As a result we don't use the word *divorce*. Up until then we had never used the term *burnout* either, for many of the same reasons. Lowell was also worried it would lead to some form of self-fulfilling prophecy. If we used it, would it suddenly be true? If we avoided saying it might we not also be able to avoid experiencing it?

We rolled our eyes at newcomers or short-termers who, in a moment of feeling overwhelmed or culture shocked or tense from new responsibilities and roles, would toss the word out casually and carelessly, saying, "We're feeling so burnt out!" There was one particular new arrival, Bonnie. She was keen and eager to join in the work. However often, when we'd ask her to do something for the benefit of the team or the ministry, she would decline. She had to protect her boundaries. She didn't want to burn out. We didn't use such vocabulary so easily. It's a sacred thing, mental health. The word *burnout* might erode that.

Lowell was overextended and beyond himself with fatigue and exhaustion. He stayed in bed for nearly a week, getting out only for meals and to engage the kids' evening and bedtime routines. Otherwise he plummeted into a strange and quiet place. He slept a lot. He ate some. He read some. People or the idea of people paralyzed him with tiredness. He did what he absolutely had to do … or at least most of it.

In the past, a good vacation had done us good. Back in 1997, we were made team leaders when our leaders went on home assignment. During that year we had some difficult decisions to make regarding the church plant. The team had decided to stop giving this baby church money. When Lowell communicated that decision to our Indian brothers, the lay leaders were furious and accused Lowell of being demon possessed. They were convinced that the previous leader, James, would never have done such a thing. That same year, our first child was born and our marriage sank to shaky new depths. While we struggled to relate to each other, I struggled to find my place on the team with a new member in our family. Who was I now?

Our team had grown from three to 12 in the space of three weeks, bringing new relational issues as well as a string of stresses trying to settle everyone in. We had planned a conference and had led a team retreat. It had all taken its toll. We were worn out and wondered if we should even stay in South Asia. *Maybe we should call it quits. Maybe we should take a job that had been offered to us at the U.S. Sending Center. Maybe we were done.* Those were the thoughts we wrestled with back in 1997.

It was at that time that we took a two week vacation to Goa, a wonderful beach resort in South India. As we rested and slept and went for long walks and played on the beach with our 9-month-old son, we were restored. God spoke into our weariness. He reminded us of His faithfulness, our calling and His promise to be near, to be our Helper and our Strength. The vacation had done its work: the Spirit of God had soothed our spirits, restored our marriage and our sense of calling. We had returned to our city renewed and ready. It was just what we had needed. It was just what the Great Physician had prescribed!

Maybe that's what we needed now. Maybe a vacation would once again right our perspectives and heal our souls. I booked train tickets to Darjeeling, made hotel reservations on the other end and saw to all the travel details. We pulled the kids out of school and off we went. For two full weeks we enjoyed the Himalayan mountains vistas. We took long walks; we ate good food; we read books; we had extended quiet times in God's word; and we drank hot tea. We played with the kids and watched a couple of good films. There was a wonderful zoo to explore, a Himalayan Mountaineering museum to see, a Tibetan Refugee Center that peaked our interest, book stores to explore. We attended an Anglican church on Sundays and found a sincere body of Christ community that reached out to us during our time there.

The kids got to ride horses around the mountain. Lowell loved going to the roof in the early mornings for extended prayer times. I had lugged my scrapbooking all the way up the mountain and I puttered away on that in the hotel restaurant at a long table with views through the windows of Mount Kangchenjunga. Our room had a wood burning stove. We curled up to that in the evenings. We felt cozy and protected, cocooned against our real lives and circumstances; it seemed the vacation was doing its work.

However at the end of our two-week vacation I realized Lowell and I still needed long naps every afternoon and some mornings as well. When I woke up to the fact that we were crawling in bed right after getting the kids to bed, it struck me that we weren't ourselves. We hadn't bounced back as we should have on a holiday. Why were we still so very tired? Why did the idea of returning home feel like a punch in the stomach? Why did the prospects of being reunited with our community back in our city seem too much? Even our best efforts to sidestep burnout weren't enough. Leaving home didn't mean leaving our emptiness.

Ironically the two most dramatic happenings of our vacation occurred on the train rides to and from Darjeeling. In the end, these two events not only helped to torpedo our rest and our holy days, even contributing in significant ways to our burnout, but they also served as metaphors of the stress placed on us as missionaries.

On the train ride up to Darjeeling we were robbed. We had been on countless train rides all over South Asia. We had our travel routine down pat. Supper was sandwiches, hard boiled eggs, bananas and maybe a cookie or two. Lowell took the kids in turn to the bathroom down the corridor while I made up the berths. Each of them crawled in to their little spaces and slept. Lowell and I would chat a little, read some and then we, too, would find our bunks and give in to the rocking motion of the train lulling us into sleep.

This train ride was no different. I never sleep all the way through the night on a train. When the train screeches to a sudden stop at each station I always wake up. I feel for my purse, find the phone, check the time, peer out the window and wait patiently for the rocking to start up again. On that particular night I awoke at four-something and then again at five-something. At four-something the routine was intact; however, at five-something my purse was not there.

I felt frantically for it. I looked under the bunk, in the space between the bunks. I felt around Lowell's head, in case he had needed it for some reason. It wasn't there. It wasn't anywhere. Lowell awoke and started looking. Our travel companions were four college boys. They saw us anxiously looking for something and joined in the search. One of the boys called my cell number. No one answered. He tried again and again. Still no one answered. We had been robbed.

Apparently a man shaved bald and wearing a brown undershirt and rolled up blue trousers had been seen looking through our compartment somewhere between 4 and 5 in the morning. When a fellow passenger enquired as to who he was looking for, he sheepishly and silently moved on, but not before taking my favorite brown purse. Of course I had slept through all of that. We had been robbed—not only of my wallet, my cell phone, my prized lipstick--but also of our rest and our excitement at the prospects of a vacation, our hope of renewal. Our expected recovery was taken as well. Our plans for healing were also stolen. I was devastated.

On the way back home after our two weeks in the mountains, the girls and I were peering out the window looking at animals. We identified monkeys and cows, goats and water buffalo, various birds, deer, dogs, pigs and sheep. And then I saw a man pick up several broken bricks from alongside the tracks. I wondered what he was up to. I was curious to see where he was going to throw the bricks. I was horrified to see he was going to throw them at the train and at our window. Before I knew it there was three loud explosive sounds and broken glass everywhere. Lowell jumped up and grabbed Adelaide from one side of me taking her to the other side of the train. I pulled Bronwynn off the seat and on to the floor, managing to grab a blanket on the way down with which to cover our bodies. The moment was long. We had no idea if there was a band of men that would suddenly raid the train. Would we again be robbed? Would we be raped and pillaged?

As it turned out, it was a one-man quest. He was finished. His work was done. Glass was everywhere. He had thrown five bricks and broken three windows. Although many on the train were covered in tiny cuts, no one was seriously injured, which seemed a miracle considering all the shards and chips and splinters of glass. We had been attacked. Our vacation trip had been attacked. Our mental health had been attacked. What little benefit the mountain holiday had afforded had also been attacked.

Later, when Lowell and I debriefed, I described the man I had seen from the moving train's window. He was bald and wearing a brown undershirt and rolled up blue pants. Even as I said it I got goose bumps! When we exited the train, we looked back at the window. There were three holes in the window where the girls and I had sat, one where my head had been higher up on the glass, two lower ones on either side where the girls had rested their little foreheads. Clearly Satan had made every effort to destroy the effects of our break, bookending it with evil. He had attempted to rob us of our expectant joy. He had attacked our shaky peace of mind and our resolve to return to our calling. God had surely protected us: that was profoundly clear. And yet even the train ride left its mark on our souls. Our holiday now had holes in it. Our vacation was violated. The ride out of burnout wasn't as simple as a 23-hour train trip to Darjeeling.

We had reached the basement. We were burnt out. And it wasn't just Lowell. It was me, too. How on earth had we gotten to this place? We had been advocates and models in taking weekly Sabbath rest, in booking two-week vacations, in getting out of the heat of summer for three to four weeks. What had gone wrong? How did we end up like this?

*   *   *   *   *   *   *   *

I thought I knew how we would end up. I thought I knew what missionaries looked like. I had seen them up close.

When I was 8 years old my parents had packed up our small family into 12 steel drums, one wooden crate and eight 70-pound suitcases with eight carry-ons. We had left northern Alberta to traverse the globe in obedience to the Great Commission with the strains of "So send I you" ringing in our ears as we headed for Pakistan. Still wearing leotards and winter coats, we were met at the Multan airport by Auntie Carol and Uncle Warren and two cousins, Wade and Scott. Those were our only "real" relatives but they weren't the only aunts and uncles to welcome us. There was Uncle Bert with his woolen Nehru's hat and Auntie Hazel wearing an American dress with Pakistani trousers underneath, Uncle Norman--ancient, kind, lopsided and Auntie Helen in her long blue cardigan, with her sparkly, wrinkly blue eyes and tightly wrapped blue head scarf. Auntie Rilla was young, vivacious. Other aunts and uncles would later surface. I watched them all not even knowing that I was.

These "relatives" were such a part of my world. They were fixtures and family. We played games with them, went out into the villages with them, went on holidays with them, worshipped with them. These aunties and uncles attended our ceremonies, our school functions, our plays, our sports events, our birthday parties. Missionaries were everywhere. How could they not shape me? My mother Joan and her older sister Carol, the famous Brown sisters, were missionaries extraordinaire. They showed me how to be a missionary woman living in Asia. They modeled how to raise children and how to delouse those same children, how to teach Western values and manners in a Pakistani context, how to feed, water, clothe and educate them. They tirelessly made lasagnas from scratch, mixing up and rolling out the noodles, cooking up the tomatoes, simmering the sauce, setting the cottage cheese over night, grating the cheddar and assembling it all and baking it in an unpredictable boxy aluminum stove-top oven–often without electricity.

Carol and Joan were unstoppable. They mended jeans, created new fashions out of hand-me-downs. They pulled out all the stops for any occasion. Christmas was a delectable spread in the middle of the Thal desert: mince meat-tarts, sugar cookies, apple pies, and bird's nest cookies all beautifully decorated.

And I would be like them!

Lowell and I met at an outreach training program in New York City. He was attending the program, learning how to reach out to and evangelize Hindus. I was doing the childcare for the families that were attending the program. We went on one date to the New York Coffee Exchange and then he left for a three-week hiatus in Kansas before flying to South Asia. I returned to Canada where I planned to take a semester off from school to stay with my parents in Three Hills, Alberta while they were on furlough from Pakistan. Lowell and I started writing letters to each other. We wrote on old-fashioned paper with old-fashioned pens. The letters increased in frequency until we were writing nearly every day. In November I got my first fax from him. I was elated.

Lowell invited me to visit him in January and I accepted his invitation. Together with his team we traveled to the beaches of

Goa and visited other workers in the capital. Three weeks into my visit we were engaged. We went ring shopping in the old city market and toasted the moment drinking tea and eating Crème Brule at the famous Imperial hotel. And then it was off to the city where Lowell lived!

I had been warned about this city. Many people had told me how backward and oppressive it was. I had heard about Hinduism and the Ganges River. I knew very little was available there. One had to be resourceful and creative and determined to live there. I had heard all of that. It was with great trepidation that I stepped off the train that first time in to the city and its particular chaos. I remember thinking it wasn't as bad as I had thought it would be. My expectations had been low. The city had showed itself to be okay, manageable, even livable. I could do it! I could live there.

During those three weeks of visiting, I asked lots of questions, I took notes, I wrote down lists of things I would bring with me. I watched how the ladies on Lowell's team conducted themselves. How they managed their time. How they raised their babies. I was curious and I was learning. I formulated opinions and planned ahead how I would look living there in the gullies and alley ways of that ancient mayhem of a city.

One afternoon Lowell took me for a boat ride on the Ganges River. We boarded the boat south of the city at Assi Ghat and made our way slowly north. The river is beautiful in the late afternoon of winter. The sun shines on the water and highlights blues and greens hidden in the polluted browns and murky blacks. It was a peaceful ride. Until we came to the burning ghat.

Hindus believe in cremation. They cremate their dead at the river's edge and then scatter the ashes on the holy Ganges. The bodies are covered in garish gold cloth, garlanded with flowers and then laid on stacks of wood. Ghee is drizzled on the body. The mourners chant, "Ram a nam a satya hai"–the name of Ram is truth. The oldest son of the deceased takes a wood torch and starts the fire. The flames are attended until the skull is heard to pop—which indicates that the spirit has been released into the afterlife.

On that afternoon as we were floating along, our boat driver rowed us unusually close to the burning ghat and, in broken *bhabu* English, he started to count the number of bodies that were burning at that time. "Von, two, tree, four, five, six, seven, eight, nine!" There were nine bodies burning along the river bank. We were close enough to smell the scorching flesh and to see the remains through the cloth and the wood and the smoke.

I started to sob. It was unbelievably surreal and graphic. In that moment the Lord said to me, "Robynn, the fire you are seeing is not the fire they are experiencing." And I knew in that moment the reality of hell like I had never known it before. My heart broke with grief and deep sorrow. I was overwrought.

Off to the side, about 15 meters upstream sitting on the steps down to the river was a tourist who was writing post cards. I couldn't believe my eyes. How on earth could she sit there, right there, next to the fires of hell and write postcards? How insensitive! How uncaring! How apathetic!

Again in that moment the Lord spoke to me. How often had I written postcards on the edge of hell, not caring that my neighbors, my co-workers, the people I passed on the streets were heading that way? Again sobs wracked my body and my soul. In that moment God called me to South Asia. In that moment, staring into those fires, I was awakened to my own responsibility to speak out the good news, to proclaim hope and truth, and to obey the Great Commission.

*　　*　　*　　*　　*　　*　　*　　*

Lowell and I were married in the quaint little town of Three Hills, Alberta on the Canadian prairie. Not knowing each other well did not deter our love for one another and our profound sense that God was leading us together and on to South Asia. After our marriage we drove across Canada and into the U.S., landing in Reading, Pennsylvania. There I attended the New Personnel Orientation of Christar where I would join Lowell as a member of the mission.

From the time I was accepted into the mission until January 11, 1995 when we arrived in the country of our calling, we spent our time preparing to leave for the mission field. As part of our pre-field training, we took classes on conflict resolution and team dynamics. We learned about working together. How to lead, how to submit, how to work out troubles, how to make decisions, how to honor one another–how to get along.

We also took a refresher course on church planting. The five stages of church planting were dissected and analyzed and thought through. We brainstormed creative ways to survey a community; we identified clever ways to connect with people, to make relationships and to develop those into true spiritual contacts. In small groups we talked long and hard about bringing the new believers together into a baby church. With great sensitivity we broached the ideas of baptism and communion. How might these things look in a Hindu culture? How might we contextualize these functions of the church to be palatable to our Indian brothers and sisters? Decisions were made on how to best train up leaders and how to inspire them to replicate themselves among a different group of people. Of course we knew these things talked out easier than they would work out, but still we felt ready to give it a try.

As part of our pre-field preparation Lowell and I enrolled in PILAT language-acquisition training course. There we explored how to learn a language and how to develop our own language learning program. We worked out sample schedules and thought how this might all work itself out in the future. We were ready to succeed in our new language.

By Gods' grace and great provision we found over 100 people that were willing to pray for us every day. We raised financial support--enough to cover our monthly needs as well as initial setup expenses.

I shopped for the things we would need to bring with us in order to set up a household in a foreign country. I bought a potato peeler and a spatula, a garlic press and potato masher. Towels given to us for our wedding were packed into duffle bags as well as two blankets, some decorations for the walls, a white tablecloth, Tupperware canisters, ziplock bags, oregano, vanilla, deodorant and toothpaste. We debated over which books, which cassette tapes, which games, which hobbies to bring. In the end, we packed our most precious things into our carry-ons: the computer, our passports, our wedding photos and all of our expectations!

Just before that last Christmas and our January departure, Lowell and I hid ourselves away at a Christian retreat center. We knew we were ready to go. The support was in; our bags were packed; the medical checkups were finished; reports were sent in to the mission; our will was signed and sealed; our power of attorney was selected. All we lacked was a commissioning prayer and a ride to the airport. Except we also knew that while our bodies and minds were trained and ready to go, our spirits still needed some attending.

While at the retreat center we committed ourselves again to God and his great mercy. Lowell and I both dedicated ourselves to the glory of God spread abroad in South Asia. Jesus was worthy of the worship of South Asia. This motivated our going. We spent hours in prayer and reflecting on Psalm 138:

A Psalm of David.
[1] I give you thanks, O Lord, with all my heart;
I will sing your praises before the gods.
[2] I bow before your holy Temple as I worship.
I praise your name for your unfailing love and faithfulness;
for your promises are backed

by all the honor of your name.
3 As soon as I pray, you answer me;
you encourage me by giving me strength.
4 Every king in all the earth will thank you, Lord,
for all of them will hear your words.
5 Yes, they will sing about the Lord's ways,
for the glory of the Lord is very great.
6 Though the Lord is great, he cares for the humble,
but he keeps his distance from the proud.
7 Though I am surrounded by troubles,
you will protect me from the anger of my enemies.
You reach out your hand,
and the power of your right hand saves me.
8 The Lord will work out his plans for my life—
for your faithful love, O Lord, endures forever.
Don't abandon me, for you made me. (New Living Translation)

We found spiritual courage to face the unknowns, the idolatry, and the distance of South Asia. God would be with us.

*   *   *   *   *   *   *   *

We arrived in the capital city of our new country, on January 11, 1995 with our five khaki Cabela's duffle bags (the modern day equivalent to the missionary barrel of my parents) and four carry-ons. Our team leader and his wife, James and Dina, met us there and together the four of us with their two little girls in tow made the overnight train trip on to our new home. We were so excited. Our hearts were ready. Lowell had been in South Asia for a year as a single man before we got married. He was anxious to return to his interrupted language studies. He was eager to begin to settle into the culture, the city, the community and our marriage. He was ready to go! I was also ready. Filled with joy at being back in Asia, I felt an immediate sense of homecoming and familiarity. This country so mirrored the Pakistan where I had grown up. The smells and sights and sounds were so familiar. This was a comforting, pleasing thing. It was good to be back!

Right from the beginning, nothing went the way I thought it would go. For starters I was shocked that our new teammates had bottled up expectations of us. On the way from the train station to their home in a rickety old taxi, James pelted us with his own exciting dreams for us: they were so glad we were there; it was so wonderful to have another married couple on the team; he could imagine that soon we would be team leaders and they would move on; we would lead the church planting project; we would eventually become the focus group leaders; Lowell was uniquely gifted to fill this role; I was a joy to have around; they were finally freed up to pursue a burden they had for the people in another state; wasn't God good?

My ears were listening as my eyes were trying to take in the strange city I was supposed to now call home. My nose was overwhelmed. James' droning voice joined the landscape and I found myself fighting waves of panic and horror. What on earth had we done?

And then everything began to go wrong. All the ways I had planned it out, our arrival, our house hunting, our language learning, our team life—none of it went according to plan. We couldn't find a house for nearly a month. When we did finally find one, it wasn't ready. They thought it would be ready in three days … and then in another three days and then a week. Finally, after living with our gracious team leaders for seven weeks, we moved in.

We tried to start our language study. Lowell had a tutor he had used before, so we made arrangements to begin meeting with him daily for lessons. Two lessons later the tutor's father died. Hindi came to a screeching halt. Our team leader knew of my childhood in Pakistan and, as a way to honor my experiences there, didn't provide the same orientation that other new workers experienced.

They assumed I knew Asia--and in many ways I did, but only weird random facts. I had no idea how to live there, how to do ministry there. We were floundering already and we hadn't even started. The team was tight-knit and close, their relationships already formed. It was hard to enter in. Six weeks after our arrival we attended a conference with the rest of our group. One afternoon Lowell went out exploring and came back to our hotel room with strawberries (an unheard of and extravagant treat). We sat on the bed and ate those precious berries with tears running down our faces. It was so very hard. This wasn't what we had signed up for. We felt lonely, threatened, useless and silenced.

We eventually settled into our new routines and calling. We learned how to live there. We figured out how to survive, how to endure, how to find joy. There were other strawberries eaten in happier circumstances under different ceiling fans. For twelve and a half years we lived year in, year out under the stresses of life in Asia. We didn't merely survive. We were in leadership over our local team and also over several teams scattered across the region. We started a profitable business and an Ashram retreat center. Together with others we also helped start local churches and an international fellowship. Lowell championed the cause of Hindus within our sending agency and we saw real changes that positively affected our work.

We hosted countless short-term missionaries and training programs. New arrivals often stayed with us for weeks on end; overnight guests were frequent; our guest room was rarely empty. Lowell and I planned various conferences and retreats and taught at many more. We welcomed new arriving workers; we packed up departing workers. Cups of coffee and tea were served on our rooftop to many, many people. Lowell counseled marriages in distress and helped guide couples not yet married. We advised more than one young family on raising children in South Asia. We answered countless phone queries about where to get something, who to talk to, what to say, which way to go. We prayed with some sick teammates, nursed and advised other sick teammates and took others to the hospital, sitting with them there. Tears and laughter were a part of most days as we walked through the strains and pains of life in the trenches with the community of faith God had established there on the banks of the Ganges.

It was a good and full, hard and intense kind of life and it took its toll. In the end it's difficult to say which straw it was that broke our fragile camel's back. Was it discovering that our trusted assistant had stolen 26,000 rupees? Was it Rajesh, plagued with demons and bipolar disorder, who camped out on our roof and virtually held us hostage for nine hours calling us profane names, slandering our character, threatening our children's lives and mocking our God, and all of that only two days after Lowell had had his appendix removed in a little known hospital in the back alley ways of our city?

Was it trying to fit into the local school's calendar year and never getting the time for a proper vacation? Was it having leadership that never asked how we were, but instead asked us how everyone else on the teams was doing? Was it simply just the accumulated affect of years of battling for water, cooking fuel, electricity, fans, safe food to eat and against disease and vermin, rodents and mosquitoes?

Was it when our landlord rented out the space below our house and gave the new tenant permission to undertake huge renovations that eventually resulted in a two centimeter crack through our daughter's bedroom, our bedroom and eventually the bathroom as well? Was it seeing their loyalty switch to the "highest" bidder as they gave in to the new tenant's wishes above ours since he had the most money to contribute? Was it when we started the reconstructive work on the Ashram and the constant stress of dealing with contractors and our landlady and Pandit Ji's irrational control?

I'm not sure which thing it was. I only know that we ended up two exhausted, weary people. We had changed. We were not who we had been before. Although we had long nights of sleep and daily naps (sometimes more than one a day) we started escaping for a couple of hours every afternoon in to the world of the *Gilmore Girls* or *Everybody Loves Raymond*.

Both Lowell and I began to dread being with people, entering into what seemed like another constant state of culture stress, even after being there all those years. The slightest interruption or change in plans overwhelmed me and made me panic. Nighttime was marked by hours of insomnia where I would lay awake and fret. Anxiety built up at alarming rates. We were perpetually exhausted, extremely critical and strangely pessimistic.

At first I thought it was just Lowell. I felt incredible pressure to keep things going while he was in what I initially hoped was a passing funk. I entertained guests, made excuses for Lowell, attended meetings or visited friends without him. He didn't feel well. It was true, and that was the excuse I used for him. A couple of kind, concerned friends in the community confronted me one day. They could see I was running in circles, denying my own indisputable state of mind, in a futile attempt to protect Lowell's.

It was during this time when we both hit rock bottom that I made the plans to escape on that much needed vacation to Darjeeling. This would be the solution. This would help us to bounce back. This would be all that we needed. I booked the train tickets, the hotel accommodations; we pulled the kids out of school and off we went.

However the enemy of our souls certainly did what he could to thwart our plans. I had had such high hopes for that time away. It had been a good break from our circumstances and yet it really hadn't accomplished all that we hoped it would. God did meet us there in that beautiful mountain town and He accompanied us back home, but I was disappointed that He didn't do the miraculous and restore us completely. When we returned from that break in April 2006 and were still in such a bad way, I knew

39

we were coming to an end. I can see now that God was bringing clarity and recognition of our need for healing.

Lowell had been pushing me to consider a longer furlough in North America. We were overdue for a break as it was. Initially we had planned on being gone a year; and I had resisted even that much time. With our kids in the local school system, missing a year would probably mean a decision to home school when we returned. Being gone a full year also seemed so disruptive to the Ashram, and to the fellowships and to our team, as well as to our relationship with our friends, neighbors and landlord's family. But it became clear that a longer time would be needed to fully recover what we had lost. Lowell convinced me and our mission leadership that we would need a two-year sabbatical. We began to make those plans.

It seemed to me that a lot of people leave the field for the sake of healing, physical and emotional. That had always annoyed me. If it was true that God was the healer, couldn't He just as easily do that healing in Asia where He was also resident? Why must people run to their mother lands to find rest? Lowell and I began to pray that God would begin our healing, if not complete it, before we even left South Asian soil.

Toward that end Lowell started to shed some of the hats he had been wearing. He transferred his leadership of the region. He made provisions for the conference that was coming up to be one where a new leader would be declared. His role in the business was given over to someone else. We found someone to take over the Ashram for the two years we would be gone, including someone to move into our house and to care for our dog. Team leadership was also eventually handed over.

Together we made the decision that I had adamantly resisted for so long to home school our oldest son. The local system wasn't meeting his needs. He didn't do well with the rote learning and the memorization of facts. Connor required a more tactile approach with more challenging reading and writing than the ESL style of language arts that was offered at our local school.

Connor is a very social child. I am a very social mother. I couldn't see how pulling him out of school and community would work for him or me, but I felt compelled to give it a try for the sake of his academic success and confidence.

I was nervous as to how this would affect me as well. I was already so very tired. How would I balance the demands of schooling on top of what was already a very full schedule? Little did I know that this decision actually forced me to slow down and stay home more. It gave me permission to not answer the phone in the mornings. It provided me the excuse to say "no" to things. In a bizarre way, it really was God's provision for the beginning of my restoration.

God did another thing that fall which forced us to put our feet up. Lowell came down with Dengue fever. Dengue starts with chills, headache, pain when you move your eyes and a low backache. There is also aching in your legs and joints. Sometimes a rash appears on your hands and feet. The fever part lasts for a variable number of days but the potential complication of internal hemorrhaging forces the patient to rest for three to four weeks. It was as if God said, "Hey, take a rest!" Three weeks into Lowell's dengue, I also came down with it. There was now the chance for me to rest. Wasn't God good?

Our time there came to a crashing close. We were scheduled to leave at the end of May. Toward the beginning of the month I broke out in a staph infection that covered my arm and moved up my neck and on to my chest and face. It was miserable. High temperatures and an unusually high humidity resulted in no healing. The usual topical medicines were no longer effective. All immunities were down. Eventually I went in to see the doctor. He prescribed antibiotics. Seven days later I was still breaking out in new blotches of staph. The doctor increased the strength of the medicine and I kept taking it for another seven days.

Meanwhile we packed up our lives into 19 Rubbermaid storage tubs. We sorted and labeled. Friends came to help clean out drawers and corners. Tricycle trolleys carried our things to the storage room in a nearby market. The electricity was typically sporadic, as were our moods and tempers. It was a mountain to summit and the climbing was strenuous. Finally the kids and I climbed in to the auto rickshaw that would take us to our closest friends, the Nicklesons, where we had planned on camping out that last week in the city. It was such a wave of exhaustion and relief, sorrow and more relief, when we tootled down the lane and out the gate. We were done. We waved goodbye to our neighbors and the shopkeepers along the way.

The last week I became quite sick. I figured the 14 days of accumulated antibiotics had wreaked their havoc on my intestines. I was up most of that last night in our house with terrific bouts of diarrhea and pain. When the auto pulled in to the Nicklesons place I got out and up into their place and collapsed into bed. By God's grace I made it through the various last events: the last church service, the last team meeting, the last meal at our favorite restaurants with friends, the last goodbye party.

At the end of the week Lowell and Connor flew to Nepal. Lowell had always dreamed of trekking to Everest Base Camp. He heightened the metaphor by tacking it on to our seven years of leadership. He had scaled the heights of vision and direction, now he would climb the heights of the Himalayas. Connor who was then 10 would accompany his dad on what would be a once-in-a-lifetime opportunity.

The day after they left, my body descended into terrible disease. With my course of antibiotics over for the rampaging staph infection, the new festering infection in my abdomen let loose. Within 12 hours the diarrhea was unstoppable. I developed a high fever. The heat, the exhaustion and the constant running resulted in a quick dehydration. I was very ill. A doctor friend came to see me and recommended that I be admitted to a hospital so that I could get on IV fluids. I was very reticent to do that, not want to subject my girls to any more disruption. I also knew from experience that having someone in the hospital is a big job; it means someone being there with the patient around the clock to provide bedside care. We were already causing so much extra work for Beth and Donnie and other friends in the city.

The doctor prescribed another round of another type of antibiotics. Four days later I was finally improving. A week later I was slowly gaining strength. Ten days later the girls and I flew out of our city. We said goodbye to our best friends, the Nicklesons; we said goodbye to our city, our favorite eateries and shopping places, our memories, our children's birth place, the place where I bought Lowell's first watch, the shop where we got Connor's first bike; we said goodbye to our home. Our dear friend Lucy came with a taxi, loaded the luggage, the girls and a still very weak me and took us to the airport.

On the way to the airport I looked out the window and wondered at what God was doing. We were broken people leaving. We were a fragile family. I wondered if we'd ever be back again. I think I even wondered if we'd ever be okay again.

Survival Tip #2
Make time to meditate

When life gets hard, when the battle is intense, and despair has made its way to a corner of our hearts, we need to refocus and take some time to spend alone with God. Meditate on God's message to us in the following passage about hardship, perseverance and eternity. We have found the Word of God to be vital in seasons of sorrow and stress. May the Holy Spirit use the Word to minister to your soul.

2 Corinthians 4:7-18 (New Living Translation)

> [7] We now have this light shining in our hearts, but we ourselves are like fragile clay jars containing this great treasure. This makes it clear that our great power is from God, not from ourselves.
>
> [8] We are pressed on every side by troubles, but we are not crushed. We are perplexed, but not driven to despair. [9] We are hunted down, but never abandoned by God. We get knocked down, but we are not destroyed. [10] Through suffering, our bodies continue to share in the death of Jesus so that the life of Jesus may also be seen in our bodies.
>
> [11] Yes, we live under constant danger of death because we serve Jesus, so that the life of Jesus will be evident in our dying bodies. [12] So we live in the face of death, but this has resulted in eternal life for you.

[13] But we continue to preach because we have the same kind of faith the psalmist had when he said, "I believed in God, so I spoke."[14] We know that God, who raised the Lord Jesus, will also raise us with Jesus and present us to himself together with you. All of this is for your benefit. And as God's grace reaches more and more people, there will be great thanksgiving, and God will receive more and more glory.

[16] That is why we never give up. Though our bodies are dying, our spirits are being renewed every day. [17] For our present troubles are small and won't last very long. Yet they produce for us a glory that vastly outweighs them and will last forever! [18] So we don't look at the troubles we can see now; rather, we fix our gaze on things that cannot be seen. For the things we see now will soon be gone, but the things we cannot see will last forever.

THREE

THE EXPLORATION CONTINUES, EXPECTATIONS OF HERSELF AND HER ROLES

People going into ministry are usually idealistic, especially
missionaries. We want to go out and change the world, to love the
world on Christ's behalf. We intend to make a difference through the
sacrifices we make. The pain of discovery that we are not as "good"
or as "loving" or as "committed" as we believe ourselves to be is very
real. It doesn't take long before we discover that we don't measure up
to our idealistic self. –Larry and Lois Dodds

Missionaries are usually idealistic about what they want to accomplish for the Lord. I remember, during Ramadan, seeing two women beggars with their children on our street. I told them to wait while I ran upstairs to get clothing that would fit their children. I was rehearsing how I would share with them the love of the Messiah even as I shared the bag of clothing I had prepared for them. I was so excited as this seemed like a perfect opportunity to meet a physical need as well as a spiritual one. As I was bringing them the bag these two women rushed toward me. One grabbed one handle of the bag and the second woman grabbed the other end. They began yelling at each other and fighting over the bag. I had thought they were friends, maybe sisters, who were walking together. Maybe they were. I tried to tell them that there were plenty of clothes for all the children. They were not listening and had no interest at that point in time in hearing of the love of the Messiah. They were too busy arguing over a bag of second-hand clothes. I left them fighting on the street as I returned, feeling deflated, to my home. I so wanted to help these women and their children.

It is our love for God as well as our love for people that feeds our desire to do good works and help others. However, reality did not match my expectations of how I was going to serve the Lord and do good to help others.

In the book *Too Valuable to Lose*, William Taylor (1997) contrasts the ministry expectations of the boomers (those born between 1946 and 1964) with busters (born between 1965 and 1983). Focusing on boomers, he reports that boomers are committed to excellence in their service and want precise ministry descriptions. Though their expectations are high, the normal overseas experience almost always falls short of what missionaries were expecting. The danger of high expectations, Taylor (1997) further noted, is that boomers are susceptible to disillusionment. However, disillusionment is not just a problem for boomers. According to the survey, missionaries of all ages have experienced disillusionment. Disillusionment that is not dealt with can help lead to burnout. One woman who completed the survey tells of her own high expectations and how she dealt with disillusionment:

> It is certainly much more difficult than I expected. I had very high expectations of myself (not necessarily placed on me by others), so when I 'failed,' I mostly 'failed' myself and not others. I had to learn to be much more fluid and flexible, even changing my own expectations. I had to rely on God to do the work, not on what I did/do. I had to also let go of perceived expectations–expectations that I thought others had of me–to focus on what God wanted me to do (confirmed through

48

prayer and Bible study, my husband, my children, etc.). I had to realize that it is a tough job and life!

Not only may many missionary self-expectations be high, they may often be unrealistic. A missionary woman who dealt with high expectations and a harsh reality is quoted by Smith (2004):

"You have to learn to merge your idealism with your reality! It's good to be idealistic, but what motivates us also creates high expectations within us, expectations of ourselves. Then we feel failure very keenly," says Connie, "I've seen this with women all over the world." (p. 28)

It is uncertain why some missionaries deal with unrealistic expectations more than others. The reasons could involve receiving a divine call for a very important task with eternal consequences, reading amazing missionary biographies with miraculous happenings, having a strong but untried faith in God who can do the impossible or experiencing such success in their home countries that missionaries automatically assume the same level of success when moving overseas. Most probably it is a mixture of all of these and more. Missionaries have a certain stereotype or picture of what a missionary should be like (Foyle, 2001). It is probably an unrealistic picture; nevertheless, missionaries may strive to be the perfect missionary without considering that the expectation may be unrealistic. An example of unrealistic expectations is given by a missionary woman on her survey when she was asked how she viewed missionaries before she became one:

I thought they [*missionaries*] always had it all together—ministry, family life, personal goals, perfect children. We only seemed to see them when stateside and doing presentations with glowing reports. I never heard about the day-to-day disappointments and failures.

Some high expectations may be realized eventually, if missionaries take into account the amount of time and effort needed. Many expectations take years to come to fruition; however, missionaries want and often expect more immediate results. Notice the adjectives that Jones (1995) uses in a list of some of these unrealistic expectations: "a desire for *immediate* fluency in the language, an *immediate* acceptance by and *close* relationship with nationals, and a *satisfying, gratifying* ministry with results during the *first few years* of service [italics added]" (p. 66). Notice what a woman reported in her survey about her expectations about language:

> I always assumed that missionaries spoke the language fluently wherever they went. This is not true. Some languages are so difficult that it is hard for a foreigner to become fluent. I feel a lot of shame that I cannot speak better than I do."

Although both men and women missionaries deal with unrealistic expectations, it would appear that women struggle with expectations more than men. This is true for both single and married women. They not only deal with many of the same personal expectations, but some additional ones as well. Single women deal with expectations of themselves regarding whether they will marry, how they think they will fit into their host culture and what roles they will have, how they will deal with loneliness and develop friendships. Read what several single women wrote about their expectations of themselves, their roles and their work:

> I had this idea that I would get off the airplane in a foreign country, not knowing or being known by anyone and being unable to speak their language—and yet somehow to begin a ministry here.

⋒ [Missionary life] is harder; [there is] more conflict; [I feel]
often unappreciated.

⋒ ... I don't really have one job description. I just fill needs
as they arise. ... The ministry is not as team-oriented as I
thought and each individual is really expected to sink or
swim on their own.

⋒ [I'm] having a very difficult time sorting out what is
personal time and ministry time. Take ministry out of
my life and what is left? Not much.

⋒ I am a person who generally works well in a structure
where I know what is expected of me. There have
been times when it has been difficult to know the
expectations.

⋒ ... [I'm] feeling discriminated against for being a single
woman. It's tough to have to do it all by yourself, and
then not having others see that! And then being looked
down upon for asking for help when that is already so
hard to do!

For married women, the problem with expectations could be
a result of their roles being multiple and less clear. Vander Pol's
(1982) research notes that women missionaries deal with more
stress than men. In a survey by Chester in 1983, 91 percent of
missionary wives as opposed to 88 percent of missionary husbands
reported they were personally more stressed or as stressed working
as missionaries than they were before becoming missionaries. He
did conclude that women experience more stress:

Although the mean tedium/burnout scores for this group did
not indicate that the members as a whole felt more stressed

51

than other professional helping groups, the wives' scores were higher than the husbands' scores in most countries and indicated that the wives were feeling higher degrees of stress. (pp. 22-23)

Other research seems to indicate the same thing. In a study by Crawford (2005) on the relationship between role perception and well-being in married female missionaries, women who were balancing their roles as mothers and missionaries were perplexed. Before arriving overseas, mothers with small children expected that they would be more involved in ministry among nationals alongside their husbands. However, they spent more time in ministry in their homes. Notice how this is shown in the lives of missionary women who responded in the survey:

"I realize I thought I would be out winning the people, leading the people or pushing the boundaries, but really I am at home taking care of the nest so my husband can do all these things. I am not sure I actually fit the profile to do church-planting work. So that just hits me in the face as well."

"I spend a lot more time just living. It was a surprise to find that I am still the same person I always was, and I do the same things I always did, just in a different setting and a different way. (Instead of throwing my laundry into the machine, I hand-launder everything.)

Instead of spending hours every day with national women, I spend hours doing things like banking, marketing, fixing broken things, arranging logistics for volunteer teams (during which time all other work stops!). I think one of the hardest things for women to adjust to is the change in their role. Most missionary women have been very involved in ministry before coming to the field. They often have been the leaders of many things in their churches, and by nature most of us are leaders and go-getters, often overachievers who need to feel like we are doing something valuable.

When these women arrive on the field they are no longer the bosses or the leaders. They are stay-at-home moms who spend an enormous amount of time keeping the house running, home schooling kids, trying to learn the language, etc. I often hear them say, 'when do I get to do ministry?' They have gone from lots of ministry to almost none. They go through withdrawal! I have seen this many times among new missionaries. It helps to have an older missionary woman to mentor them and explain that this is a stage in life; our ministry opportunities change as our family changes.

I never anticipated the extent to which I would become a 'homemaker,' having always worked outside the home prior to cross-cultural service. The loss of personal identity and being viewed more as 'my husband's wife' was unexpected and unsettling on a personal level. I had assumed that I would find meaningful work that suited my particular skills, but that has rarely been the case. Women who are gifted at working with children or with women's groups seem to have the easiest adaptation in terms of finding their role.

Balancing roles as a married missionary woman with children seems to be a significant issue. In the book *Missions in Contexts of Violence*, Smith (2008) wrote a chapter using case studies of missionary women. She gave the illustration of Vivian, who was struggling with her expectations as a missionary and mother. She had three small children and hosted 150 guests in three weeks. The issue for her was not the overload of work as much as expectations. "The problem was not having too many guests or having the wrong things on her list, she realized, as much as it was that she had personal expectations for herself and her life which could not be met" (p. 117). Vivian had to release her expectations of how life should be and accept what was. One can sense the struggle she had trying to balance her role as a wife, mother and missionary because she wanted to succeed in every area. She expected to be able to do it all and found it difficult, if not impossible. Smith (2008) also points out that women struggle with what they think they should do (expectations) and what they want to do (reality). There is apprehension that they are being idle or ineffective if they do what they want and not what is expected.

Whether a woman is single or married, I cannot imagine hosting 150 people in three weeks without some struggles. I would think, yes, anyone hosting 150 people in three weeks should think it hard to do because it is! I think many missionary women like Vivian do amazing things every day and they do them well. And yet, they somehow think they aren't doing enough or should do more or do things better. Is there room for improvement for all of us in what we do and how we serve? Probably so at times, but to do what we do at all is sometimes miraculous in itself! It is easy to see how unrealistic or high expectations of oneself could help lead missionaries to disillusionment and burnout. Simply reading Robynn's story in chapter two and recalling some of her expectations and experiences highlight the role that expectations can play in burnout. Some of the unrealistic expectations can never be met no matter how hard one keeps working. If she keeps working to try to meet these expectations, she will wear herself out. It might well be that the missionary woman's unrealistic self-expectations are her worst enemy.

Other women who responded to the survey share some of their expectations of themselves and their roles in ministry:

◯ "Before coming to the field, I thought we would get here and lead nationals to Christ, but after coming, at times I have felt that I didn't really know how to do it or what to do to get started."

◯ "I didn't expect the opposition of the devil (spiritual warfare) would be so intense in this process, nor did I understand fully how to combat it spiritually. I have discovered that 'success' in my ministry is directly related in proportion to how much time I devote in developing my personal relationship with the Lord, growing spiritually through Bible study, my quiet time with Him, my prayer time and getting others involved in praying for us. I thought working cross culturally was all about doing lots of work, but I find it's more about being. Being in Christ, listening to His leading and letting Him flow out to minister to those I am serving. Another aspect I did not expect was all the 'hard work slogging in the trenches' (doing pre-evangelism), the fierce opposition and resistance of the people, with only two people coming to know the Lord as their Saviour through my husband's witness, after seven years. I didn't think we wouldn't have problems, but I just never anticipated how hard it would be to get the opportunity to witness and share my faith without a lot of hostility and suspicion."

◯ "I have been blessed with the joy of seeing God use my training and abilities in ways that I had never dreamed could be done on the mission field. I have seen God's wonders and have been in awe of what He can do. When we first got to our first mission field, there were some ministries that I was expected to be part of. However, I was aware of my limitations and knew that it was my own responsibility to seek God's priority for my life. I could not transfer that responsibility to others and let their expectations be my priorities. So I can say that God has done much more than I could ever expect. He has been faithful in every way and has honored me with the joy of seeing Him work."

In thinking through what some of these expectations are and what I have personally experienced or witnessed, I developed a survey consisting of a list of 34 expectations. Missionary women were asked to put a 1 (rarely), 2 (sometimes), 3 (often), or a 4 (always) corresponding to what they expected of themselves. Then, they were to look through the list again and rate what actually corresponded to their reality. According to the results of this survey, women's expectations almost always exceeded their reality. Note in the chart below the expectations that are listed and the percentage of women whose expectations were higher than their reality, equal to and less than their reality.

Expectation	Percentage of expectations greater than reality	Percentage of expectations that equal reality	Percentage of expectations less than reality
1. Have a daily quiet time	57.5	41.0	1.6
2. Have a best friend on my team	50.2	30.0	19.8
3. Embrace my new host culture	50.9	42.9	6.2
4. Am fruitful	75.4	21.5	3.1
5. Am growing spiritually continually	67.6	30.2	2.2
6. Have a successful family life	56.5	38.5	5.0
7. Am a prayer warrior	70.4	25.2	4.4
8. Enjoy national friendships	48.6	39.3	12.1
9. Have a strong relationship with my supporters.	50.5	39.9	9.7
10. Stay connected with my sending church	49.8	41.4	8.8
11. Am a good public speaker	30.4	39.2	30.4
12. Teach well	35.3	38.5	26.2
13. Am spiritually dynamic	62.7	28.2	9.2
14. Am brave and unafraid of new circumstances	43.2	41.6	15.2
15. Have good leadership in my organization	42.9	38.6	18.5
16. Have a strong team	50.2	35.5	14.4
17. Continually trust God for everything	65.8	30.1	4.0
18. Have a sure and certain calling to my work	27.3	62.4	10.2
19. Persevere no matter what	31.1	48.8	20.2
20. Have high standards for myself and my family	25.8	60.1	14.2

21. Do not experience burnout	43.0	36.1	20.9
22. Am a strong leader	39.1	39.1	21.9
23. Have miraculous stories to tell of how God is using me	55.1	35.8	9.0
24. Do not fail	50.0	36.3	13.8
25. Am admired by people for my calling	17.6	42.0	40.4
26. Am well cared for by my organization	24.2	46.6	29.2
27. Am accountable to leaders in my church and organization	39.4	47.5	13.0
28. Succeed in every area of life	49.8	34.3	15.9
29. Am well balanced in areas of ministry in and out of home	56.0	36.2	7.9
30. Am certain about my roles and able to do them all well	47.8	40.1	12.1
31. Am content without a lot of money	34.6	48.9	16.5
32. Sacrifice my happiness for my husband's ministry	33.1	47.9	19.1
33. Am a trail blazer	41.3	38.8	20.0
34. Feel confident in ministry	45.3	40.1	14.6

Note that for these missionary women the biggest gaps between expectations and reality were in their own spiritual life with areas of fruitfulness, prayer and spiritual growth. Women headed to the mission field would likely be women of prayer (or at least women who believed prayer was a good idea) and were probably experiencing a degree of fruitfulness and spiritual growth in their home culture. The survey shows missionary women clearly expect to experience these things even more abundantly in their full-time ministry overseas. However, moving and adapting to a different culture, coupled with the spiritual warfare involved certainly takes its toll in every area of spiritual life and ministry. More than one missionary woman—or at least one (me!)—has gone overseas thinking that crossing the ocean and becoming a missionary will make her more spiritual. It eventually does as she perseveres and keeps walking by faith in the Lord. However, the process usually involves conviction, pain and hard work through turmoil. It is harder to live overseas. It takes more time to clean, cook and shop. Support systems are not as prevalent in a new place, especially in the beginning. There is language study, culture shock, homesickness, team dynamics and sometimes physical ailments such as diarrhea, new viruses and illnesses, often in the midst of extreme heat or cold. A missionary woman gets tired, both physically and spiritually. When her expectations are high for spiritual growth and reality isn't measuring up, guilt is added to the equation and then more guilt for feeling guilty.

It is important to identify what our expectations are and evaluate them. Looking at the areas where the biggest gaps are, let's explore the third highest one, that of growing spiritually, Recognizing the difficulty of growing spiritually even in our home country, if we aren't having a close walk with God there, the odds dramatically increase that we won't overseas—even if we are called "missionaries." When we desperately need the Lord the most, it seems often hardest to connect with Him. We know we need to have an intimate walk with the Lord, but it seems harder to come by when simply surviving takes up so much time! We need to recognize that life—especially our spiritual life—will not be easy, and to go prepared and ready for the struggle of maintaining our walk with God.

There is no magic formula for connecting with God. I don't believe it will ever be easy. I remember asking a godly woman in her 80s when spending time with God becomes easy. She replied that it must be sometime after 80! It is vital to recognize that it will take time to learn the language, time to plant seeds and see fruit develop and time spent connecting with God. At times I was driven out of necessity to seek God. At other times it was all I could do to read His Word and pray. In seeking to spend time with God, depending on seasons in my life, I've planned to be in His Word and to pray every other day, five days a week, when kids were sleeping or when they were awake. I've prayed showering, walking, kneeling, standing, doing dishes or pacing the floor. I've used devotional books, done word studies and read Old Testament and New Testament books one at a time. Creativity in spending time with Him, listening to Him or resting while we wait on Him is vital as women with varied roles and schedules. In our early years overseas I remember seasons where Bible study was essential to me and times when I just had to pray more and spend time talking with God. It wasn't that one was more important than the other, but at times it seemed I needed more of one than the other. We've all experienced dry times as well as times of spiritual revival in our hearts. Spiritual growth takes time and the more we grow the more we want to grow! It is vital to pursue our walk with God. I can't have idealistic views of what spirituality should be like based on others' lives, but need to keep growing spiritually as He works in me.

The reason I chose this expectation to explore is because the time we spend with God has a bearing on whether we burn out or not. Of women who have their devotions consistently, only nine percent burn out—that's one in ten women. However, when women do not have a regular quiet time with God, the number increases to 32 percent—three in ten women. That is a marked difference. For those women who were consistent in spending time with God and growing spiritually the odds dramatically decrease that they will burn out. Could it be that time of quiet is needed to regain focus on what is truly important for us to do? Is it the supernatural strength and closeness with God, that abiding in the vine, which enables us to work well and wisely? Spending time with God is crucial for our spiritual health, emotional health and long-term fruitfulness in cross-cultural ministry.

Each expectation we have of ourselves needs to be recognized, evaluated and either discarded or committed to work on for progress. Often the biggest problem is that the expectations are never identified until they are unmet. Even going through the survey list of 34 expectations and thinking through them is helpful. Quite a few women in the survey had fours marked for every expectation for herself. They expected they should be able to do everything perfectly! Women often don't (and can't) meet their own expectations.

Although a review of the literature yields examples of what missionary women expect from others and what is expected from them, an area of even greater importance is that of perceived expectations. Every expectation that a missionary woman has needs to be evaluated to determine if it is real or perceived. Some expectations people have in ministry do not come from others, but from themselves (Sanford, 1982). These expectations are thought to be what others expect, but in reality they are self-generated and only perceived to be true.

Missionary women may feel that others expect perfection, when in reality this is only a perceived expectation. For married women, there is a "super mom" myth with which missionary women struggle (Hawkins, 1994). She stresses, "One of the most important steps in surviving the stress of missionary life is to overcome the 'super mom' myth. Many women feel that to do God's will in a foreign field they must strive for perfection" (p. 3). A missionary woman's best defense is to examine expectations like "super mom," judge their validity and deal with them accordingly. She must think through all such expectations and ask herself not only where the expectation comes from, but also if it is even possible to attain. Another step is to also look to God, asking Him what His expectations are of her. We can do this through prayer and Bible study. Looking at scripture was extremely helpful to me when we were overseas during our second term. I was feeling pressure as I looked at expectations I had of myself as well as what I thought others might be expecting of me.

I did a Bible study looking at women in scripture, what their roles were, how they ministered and what was written about them. That was a turning point for me in determining where and how to invest my time according to what I saw from scripture as God's expectations of me.

A woman who filled out the survey remarked how she encourages women to think about whether their own expectations are realistic or not:

> I tend to place high expectations and standards upon myself. I've remarked that women seem to place upon themselves unreal expectations. Generally, as a supervisor, I constantly ask women to carefully consider what unreal expectations they might have or feel that others are imposing upon them. Then we look at what reality is. Women like to be everything to everyone, make everyone else happy. They need help in sorting out the meaningful from the non-essential.

So not only do missionary women need to determine which standards are realistic and which are not; there is also the need to deem what is essential and what is not. It is only as women intentionally think through their goals and standards that unrealistic goals can be set aside without guilt so that those that are realistic and essential can be focused on and achieved for the glory of God.

Survival Tip #3
Release Expectations

When my children were little I (Sue) thought I knew what they would be like as they grew up. I somehow thought they would be versions of me and their dad in smaller bodies. As time went on I realized that God made them with different personalities, gifts and abilities from what I had imagined. Looking back, I think I imagined them growing up to be all I never was and wanted to be. I hadn't ever thought about the expectations I had for my children. I couldn't verbalize them because I didn't even know I had them until they weren't met.

I had a picture in my mind that I later drew on paper in my prayer journal as a reminder to me as I prayed for them. I dug four graves and intentionally buried my expectations of my children and released them so that God could fulfill His expectations in them.

That is what we need to do with our expectations of ourselves. It could be you need to have a funeral, maybe not for all of them. Maybe so. Write them out one by one. "I expect to be superwoman able to do it all." Cross over it with a pen and bury it. "I expect to be married." "I expect to (you fill in the blank)." Put crosses on the graves. Let the expectations go. Then look to God. What does He want to do in us and through us? What guidelines do we find in Scripture? What godly counsel are we receiving? Where have we been unrealistic in what we are expecting of ourselves? We must recognize the fierceness of the spiritual battle we are in and the fact that, if we are busy expecting to handle everything ourselves, we are not looking to God. We need to depend on God and not ourselves.

After the funeral of our expectations, after the grieving of what we feel we have lost, we are ready to experience God in who we are. To be—in Him; not always doing, working, striving. To let Him help us determine who we are and our course of action, not who we think we "should" be or attempting to do all that we think we "should" do.

I thank God that my children are who they are, that God made them the way that He has and gifted them to serve Him in their own unique ways. I'm thankful that out of the buried expectations He resurrected and renewed my hope in Him.

I also thank God for making me the way that He has. I don't have all the spiritual gifts, talents and abilities in the world. Neither do you. We cannot and should not expect to. That's why He put us in His body. We need each other. We need Him.

Do you need to have a funeral service to attend for some of your expectations?

FOUR

THE EXPLORATION CONTINUES, EXPECTATIONS AND HER SENDING AGENCY

"Upon reflection it became apparent that both he and the mission organization expected him to perform at "super normal levels." –
Jarrett Richardson

Having served both overseas and in the U.S. office of a sending agency, I have the perspective and understanding of the challenges and blessings of both arenas. I remember living overseas and nervously awaiting a visit from our "home office" leader. What would he say? Am I in trouble? Is my house clean enough? I also have gone to visit missionaries as a "home office" leader, and have heard them say they were nervous before we came. My main goal was to be an encouragement, a blessing, a help to my co-workers. I had no intention to judge or criticize. I intensely dislike the "us vs. them" mentality that can exist between the missionary and the mission agency; though I think I can understand it, I would love for it to end. We are all seeking to work together, but at times, misunderstandings and hurt can develop between the missionary and her agency due to infrequent or unclear communication, expectations, confusion and disagreements.

I found this chapter a difficult one to write. There are issues to be addressed, but there are good things happening as well between mission agencies and the missionary women who join them. Overall, according to the survey, women missionaries seem pleased with their mission agencies and have seen progress in how the agencies are caring for their women. They are very thankful for the care and training they receive from their sending agencies. When women were asked to numerically rate how well they were cared for by their organizations, there wasn't a huge gap between expectations and reality. Forty-seven percent of the women's expectations for being well cared for by their organization equaled their reality, whereas only 24 percent had expectations higher than what they were actually experiencing. When asked about good leadership there was a bigger gap in that only 39 percent were experiencing what they expected and 43 percent were dissatisfied with their mission leadership. These figures are in very close alignment so there is a lot that is right in what missionary women expect from their agencies and how mission agencies are training and caring for their women members. However, there are also some things that need to be addressed so that even greater progress can be made.

Mission agencies seek to mobilize those who have been called into missions to help them actually get overseas for ministry, equipped and ready to serve. In order to recruit new missionaries, mission agencies present the various needy areas of the world and explain how people's gifts and abilities would enable the gospel to spread to those who have yet to hear about Jesus Christ. When trying to prepare recruits for ministry, missionaries tell true stories about amazing things God is doing around the world. However, if this is all recruits hear there may be a significant chasm between their expectations and the reality of what their missionary experience will be. Dodds (1997) noted that one young pastor, feeling misled by his mission agency, asked, "Why do they insist on teaching us in our mission training that we can bond totally with the people we go to serve? We find that impossible because the cultural gulf is too great, and so we feel guilty all the time. Can't they be more realistic?" (p. 13). It must seem to some missionaries, both married and single, that the reality of their ministry overseas is so different from what they were told to expect that they feel deceived by the mission agency that helped them to go.

Single women have felt some disparity in what they expected from their agencies regarding how they are treated as compared to how married women are treated. The first issue is that of being heard. Some single women expected the same standards to apply to them and married women; but they have felt that married women have more of a voice in the organization since they can talk to their husbands who then talk with the leadership of the mission. One single woman mentioned her need at times of male advocates:

> Female singles aren't listened to and my experience has been that I've had to use a male advocate to help in time of need ... Sometimes we're also seen as having nothing to do so we can just babysit others' kids!

Because of having mostly male leaders, one single suggested that a more deliberate step is needed to hear what the singles are saying. Maybe there could be more representation by singles to leadership in the organization. Singles need to be empowered to speak up and to keep moving through the organizational leadership flow if they feel they are not being heard. However, other singles felt their voice was more heard than their married co-workers. This issue of being heard might also be due to a personality or age factor rather than totally a marital issue. However, mission agencies need to work to be intentional to listen and interact with single women missionaries. Here are a few comments from single missionaries regarding their relationship to their organization:

♎ Job descriptions in the USA are always different on the field–things change so quickly from there to here and so many of those in the USA (organization) don't understand/have forgotten the challenges of living alone on the field.

♎ It's tough being an older single female. I'm not sure I'm seen as capable as my single male counterparts [by my organization].

Secondly, some singles thought more was expected of them than married women and that married women had more freedom in use of time, more holidays, less structure. Single women sometimes felt pressure to work too many hours since they "don't have home responsibilities." However, it must be noted that they do have home responsibilities and things they must be encouraged by their agency leadership to take care of, so there is also a need for them to set boundaries for personal time and for care of their homes. One survey respondent wrote, "Mission [agencies] in general are not single-friendly. Much more is expected from singles than marrieds." Another single also addressed the issue of more being expected from singles:

> Much more is expected from singles than marrieds. Singles have to stick rigidly to rules such as holidays, whereas families seem to always be having time off if they live in the city or if boarding school isn't far away it's any excuse to go see kids. (That I understand but treatment is different.) Singles are expected to do everything in their weekends–shopping as well as get a little rest.

Another single observed over the years that if a woman is single it can be automatically expected by leadership that she has a high energy level, is always free to host company, go the extra mile in ministry and can work many more hours than her married woman counterpart. Women are individuals, married or not, and each has her God-given capacities and gifts. Some singles enjoy having a roommate, but it should never be assumed that her apartment would be the bed and breakfast for short-term gals and guests who are coming to visit. It is sometimes the case that an older single woman prefers to have a roommate, but she may reach a point where she needs to establish a home of her own, not to the exclusion of the occasional guest but not a guest house, either. Some singles have high energy levels and can invest much more time in ministry activities. Some don't. It doesn't diminish the importance of their contributions to ministry. It's simply a matter of recognizing boundaries and living within them. Some leaders may have a very difficult time understanding their boundaries. The married woman can "retreat" when she needs to because her husband "covers" for her, but the single oftentimes has no one to stand up for her needs. Singles also don't have a "family" to acknowledge special occasions or accomplishments. People say that the "team" is the person's family but that, sadly, is oftentimes felt to be far from the truth.

Another single woman wrote of two categories when she expected and needed help from her mission leadership. The first were times of crisis when things with her teammates or projects were going poorly, and the second were times of forming new projects or teams and she needed some guidance.

The agency was helpful in times of crisis when things were going poorly, but in her first four years of experience, that help only came after things were already going poorly with the teammates and it was sort of "too late" to try to mend the problems. It may have been that the agency was more involved, but from her perspective at the time, it didn't seem that way. More timely and more proactive help was expected from her agency.

Now after 17 years of experience, she knows to ask for help and as a result she gets more help from the agency. She has found that she has to take the initiative. Some leaders can be reactive and not proactive in giving guidance. Other leaders are more assertive. So, a lot depends on the leader, especially because she is a single missionary. This makes her all the more concerned as to who her leader is and how he leads.

In the area of leadership, one single felt there was no real place for single women to use their gifts of leadership in the mission. She thought that it is essential that single women have the opportunity to influence decisions and also get training in leadership. If this isn't happening, then mission agencies are not taking full advantage of their personnel or utilizing their giftedness. She noted that unless women, single and married, are able to take the leadership positions, there is disparity.

One single also suggested that agencies should give training to better prepare marrieds to interact with single teammates. It's hard enough for a single to be constantly misunderstood as to why she's single by those in her adopted culture; she doesn't need team members making jokes about her singleness or talking down to her. Singles are sometimes given a lot of responsibility in ministry because they don't have the same responsibilities in the home, and yet they can still be treated like university students with university age-appropriate interests or desires. Single missionaries desire to be respected by their teammates. I have heard of orientation training for singles and for those who are married, but it would be helpful to have training for marrieds and singles regarding their interaction at a team level.

Regarding married missionary women and their expectations of their sending agency, the biggest area of concern for them seems to be that what they were told in orientation is often dramatically different from what they experience on the field. For example, some of the married women surveyed were told they would be in ministry with their husbands. They expected a partnership in ministry, working side by side with their husband. In their reality, however, they were often in their homes with their children while the mission looked to their husband for ministry results and reports.

The time it takes to simply live in a different culture is sometimes overwhelming. Add to that language study, visiting and day-to-day responsibilities and it is easy to feel nothing is done well. The married missionary women's roles were varied and not always clear; expectations of them by their mission agency were vague. Often times the expectations from the mission agency are intentionally vague to allow for flexibility in caring for the home, but many women felt they needed more guidance and support from their mission agencies. There seems to be a need for validation of their roles, gifts and contributions, as well as better preparation and clarification regarding the variety of what actual husband and wife partnerships may look like in missions.

It is easy to see that some married missionary women experienced cross-cultural ministry very differently from what they heard it would be like from their mission agencies. Three married missionary woman share their experiences:

> I actually bought the implied line that my husband and I would be working together, side by side, to raise our kids overseas and be missionaries together. The reality is that 'they' expect me to be the main child-raiser, and make the sacrifices necessary to enable my husband to work outside the home. While they also expect my husband to help me make it possible to do at least 10 hours of mission work a week, is that really side-by-side or even? For example, we were at a training conference and the speaker (male) freely admitted that a large [part of the] growth of Christianity in another country ... was [the result of work]done primarily by the husbands, since the wives were at home "making it possible." As someone who was an engineer making million-dollar decisions

before I came here, being funneled into a support role with little direct impact was a real shock.

🔘 I expected to have more clearly defined goals and expectations outlined for me personally by my supervisors. I came to find out very quickly that most expectations were for my husband alone. I was given flexibility, even though I had no kids at the time, in order to prioritize my time between my family and my home. However, this flexibility felt more like lack of value for the gifting I brought to the mission.

🔘 I think that my number one difficulty emotionally has been the expectations [on the part of the organization], and my not meeting them. And some of them have been expectations that I put on myself, probably. But the fact that people like me aren't referred to, ever, by our organization, makes me feel that it's mostly their expectations, and not my own, that aren't being met. If I felt affirmed in what little I can do, I wouldn't feel as badly; but wives that can't produce are ignored. The organization wants impressive results; I can't give them.

A mission agency has the opportunity to create both freedom and accountability by clarifying the married missionary woman's role as a missionary and as a wife and/or mother. Not addressing expectations only makes the situation worse for her. I like referring to prioritizing these multiple roles that many married women missionaries have as "embracing the blessed chaos." Things are chaotic; but there is great blessing in the midst of it all. Because of the variety of roles a married missionary woman has, especially when there are children at home, there will probably always be some confusion about where to invest her time. She has ministry both in her home and outside of it; the difference is the amount of time she can invest in each one. Each woman has different energy levels; the children have different personalities, learning styles and needs; there are different personalities, gifts and abilities. Mission organizations must show they value missionary women who are wives and mothers by discussing with them what their roles are and what is expected of them. They can encourage these women by helping them and their spouses clarify their roles, expectations and ministry experience.

Organizations can have a huge impact on married missionary women during orientation training by helping husbands understand their role in facilitating language learning and ministry opportunities for their wives. Husbands and wives both need to learn the language; wives desire and need time away from the home to minister to neighbors and friends as well as personal time just to be alone for awhile. Husbands should be encouraged to consider what their expectations are of their wives, and to communicate with them about these expectations so that they can work through them together. Everyone needs to be reminded that women's work and roles overseas are more challenging than in their home country. Mission leaders must urge husbands and wives to talk about sharing the work load and what it will take to live and work together as a family cross-culturally. Balancing roles, though often talked about by women missionaries, is also a key issue for missionary husbands to consider as they look at their roles as husbands, fathers and missionaries. Too many missionary wives felt that their husbands were gone doing ministry while they were left at home, fulfilling the ministry with their children alone. Husbands need to make sure they are fulfilling their responsibilities as husbands and fathers as well as missionaries. Husbands' and wives' roles and expectations need to be revisited regularly as children grow and opportunities for ministry change. Couples can do this separately and then together as they develop their ministry plans each year and evaluate how the past year has gone. Both husbands and wives have necessary and vital ministry in their homes as well as outside of it and both need to work together in determining how their time is being invested in each area of ministry.

It might be best to copy what women missionaries themselves said on the returned surveys in order for mission agencies to get a sense of some of their frustrations with their agencies regarding their roles in their different areas of ministry:

> I expected to be trained and encouraged. I never expected to take a backseat and become 'the spouse.' After over 10 years on the field, I have learned to be about what God has called me to whether or not that is ever publically affirmed or encouraged by our leadership.

> [*I would appreciate my agency*] providing me real opportunities for service and acknowledging my unique role on the field. I am concerned and frustrated when only men in our organization are invited to strategy meetings/retreats. It is practical, but leaves the obvious impression that women are valued, but not needed in direct missionary work.

> I think our organization is weak in enabling women with small children in ministry. I think it is common for ladies in this situation to feel the weight of expectations (full-time language learning or reaching a language level or having a certain number of local relationships) but have no idea how to make it happen ... there are ways for ladies in this stage of life to be engaged in ministry without sacrificing their family, but they shouldn't just be left to figure it out on their own. Recently our organization has begun focusing on better equipping women for ministry and opening up region-wide dialogue between women for sharing ideas and encouragement.

◍ I definitely need grace, but give me high expectations, too ... if I need to turn a report in, I need to turn it in by the due date. I know that's not a terribly big deal, but I wish the environment at my mission agency had a more professional feel, although I wouldn't trade the family feel for a million dollars. So, how do you have both?

◍ Where they have not met my expectations is in impressing us with the idea that we are a 'unit' while we are in training, but once [we] get to the field, we are no longer a unit and the man is to make all decisions and make all communications with those up the chain of command–which is almost everyone. ... I do agree the husband is the head of the household and he is our team leader, but sometimes the leadership can get a bit carried away with their ideas about who does what. We just continue to get it done and it doesn't really matter who wrote what in the end, as long as God is glorified and we get the job done.

◍ We receive mixed messages from our leadership. On the one hand they are supportive of homeschooling and family needs, but on the other hand they push ministry and language, so it is hard to get a clear picture of expectations. It is possible that expectations vary considerably from person to person in our company leadership.

As we read through these comments it is evident that some married women are not feeling as supported by their agencies as they would like. Agencies should be concerned that women may feel underutilized, underappreciated and yet overworked. It appears they feel less valued by their organization than their husbands. Though the issue of women in leadership will not be addressed adequately or solved by this book or probably any other, it is clear that there needs to be communication from mission leaders to the women in their organization, acknowledging their contributions to the overall goals of their mission.

Feeling unacknowledged by their organizations, according to the survey was an issue for both single and married women. In a questionnaire conducted only within my own agency in 2005, one of the top five needs missionary women have is to feel respected. They were communicating that they needed to be recognized; respect would help them feel they and their contributions are had not been feeling valued and appreciated. This need for respect is closely followed by the need for encouragement, mentoring and to be heard and wisdom as well as freedom in balancing roles. If there is no reporting from women to their leaders, they feel as if their ministry (both in the home and out of the home) is devalued and not appreciated by their mission agency. If there is no guidance, how can a missionary woman determine if she is being as effective as possible in any of her roles? It is true that a woman needs freedom in determining where to invest her time; but she also needs and wants accountability.

Mission organizations ought to consider and clearly communicate what life and ministry is actually like overseas so that all missionaries, and women in particular, can be as prepared as possible. Mission agencies would be wise to regularly evaluate how they present what ministry will look like for both singles and for married couples with and without children, as well as their expectations of workers and strategies for mobilization. Taylor (1997) emphasizes this need when he warns that that mission advertisements may conflict with expectations of new missionaries who have responded to the ads. Mission agencies ought to evaluate what they are communicating about short-term trips, as well as what picture is being presented for long-term missions. Missionaries speaking to potential candidates also need to reflect on what stories they are telling and whether they include successes and failures, joys and challenges, the miraculous and mundane. I remember one week being in London with leaders helping to plan a multi-organizational conference and the next week I was home mopping the floors. There are amazing opportunities as well as tedious chores that have to be done by men and women in missions.

Mission agencies and their leadership may be unrealistic about how long it will take to be fruitful in overseas ministry and as that is communicated, it could affect missionary expectations. Mission agencies should be discussing the values of faithfulness and fruitfulness, perseverance and effectiveness with missionaries and potential missionaries. I think one of my own biggest challenges was trying to figure out if we weren't successfully planting a church in a resistant area because God was teaching us to be faithful and to persevere even when ministry was seemingly unfruitful, or if we were doing something wrong and needed to change strategies to be more effective. It is possible that it was both. We needed to try new strategies and we needed to persevere. Mission agencies can give guidance to missionaries who are struggling with this tension through providing resources in orientation programs about perseverance and long-term commitments, as well as ongoing training on effective church planting. Married missionary women with children especially need ongoing training throughout their careers as their roles change significantly with the ages of their children.

The question of what role the mission agency plays in promoting some of these unrealistic expectations must be asked and answered. There has been too much attrition in many agencies for there to be ignorance regarding the role of expectations in attrition and burnout. Taylor (1997) points to this danger of expectations for long-term missionary service as well when he reports, "It is difficult to estimate the degree to which false or conflicting expectations contribute to missionary loss, but any experienced mission administrator is aware of the frequency with which this topic arises in discussion with missionaries concluding their service" (p. 222). Jones (1995) is in full agreement that there is a problem of unrealistic expectations as she reports one missionary's experience who left the field to return home before his first term of service was over: "I found that the missionary 'success stories' are very rare exceptions to the overwhelming mass of routine or unsuccessful activities of the missionary's day" (p. 69). Mission agencies are not unaware of the problem of unrealistic expectations and must be intentional in preparing missionary women for the miraculous and the mundane of cross-cultural ministry.

Along with the mission agency's presentation of what missions is like, there is the leadership factor in the organizational structure, which produces even more expectations from newer missionaries, male or female, about what leadership should be like. Some are looking for directive leaders; some want mentors; others are looking for shepherd/pastors. It might be good for leaders themselves to request feedback from women in their organization regarding what they want and look for in leadership and how leaders could be more helpful to women members, directly as leaders, through the organizational structure or regarding their reporting systems.

After reading through the comments on the surveys, it is apparent to me that though leadership style is important, it is knowing that they are cared about that is more important to women. They can learn how to relate to different leadership styles; they can adapt and become more assertive when needed. What is really hard to work with is thinking that mission leadership doesn't seem to show care for or value women or their ministry. I know that mission leaders value their women missionaries; however, this needs to be communicated more clearly and in more tangible ways. This can be done through listening to them, asking questions about their roles and ministry, requesting reports from them so they can communicate about their involvement and then affirming them in their overall contribution to the goals of the mission agency. If women know they are considered valuable to the task of world evangelization and if they clearly see their role in it, they can be more loyal co-workers who are able to endure challenges for the glory of God. If they don't know, we will be more likely to lose them.

When it comes to caring for mission members, most mission leaders are busy. There is almost always more to do than there is time to do it. The question mission leaders must ask themselves is how can they still show support and care even when missionaries seem to be doing well. It is easier, or at least necessary, to act when there is a crisis or challenge, but women missionaries expect to be cared for even if there aren't any problems. At times it is nice to be visited when things are going well and to be able to share about good happenings. One woman commented about how this lack of caring visits affected her:

> ... and the sense from the organization that they really don't care about us, or that they are just too busy. I don't need my hand held ... I don't need someone checking up on me every day, but it would be nice to know we haven't been entirely forgotten. I suggested to our (regional leader) that he come see us ... or rather that we hadn't seen him in a while ... and would like to. His response? 'You haven't seen me because you haven't needed to!' In other words, his world comprises such a vast area where he is consistently putting out fires, and since we aren't on fire, he doesn't need to be here.

With leadership on a team level, there is the expectation of having caring team leaders. Team leaders often try to balance following policies and showing grace. Some people may expect more grace. Others expect stricter policy. Some leaders lean towards giving more grace and others are there to make sure the policies are followed. Robynn shares her "Calculator Furlough" story where she felt policy won out over grace:

It was time to plan for our furlough. We had been in South Asia for over two years. Normally we wouldn't have thought of furlough until after having been on the field for four years, but it seemed good to us to begin to plan it out. We had arrived in South Asia in January 1995. We knew our teammates and leaders were going to be away from April 1999 through September 2000. It made sense to try to stagger our departures so that not everyone was gone from the city at the same time.

My grandparents were celebrating their 60th wedding anniversary with a family reunion in August of 1998. Couldn't we please leave for furlough July 1998 and stay until August 1999? And couldn't we also still take our planned time away from the hot plains and go to the mountains for the month of June 1998? And then wouldn't it make sense for us to simply leave for furlough from the hills? Technically it would mean being gone from our city for longer than a year, but who wants to stay in the heat during the month of June and who wants to come back to the hot summer temperatures before the monsoons have started?

We had it all sorted out in our minds and we approached our leadership asking for permission. I will never forget the meeting where we laid out our hearts and our plans. Two calculators were pulled out and our lives somehow became a mathematical equation. Days we had been on the field were tallied against days we had been off the field. There was a mission-wide formula to be followed. We had arrived on January 11. *Thirty days hath September, April, June, and November; of 28 there is but one, and all the rest have 31.* Of course we had been back to the U.S. to attend a required training program in 1996 for two months. Did that count as time on or off? Technically the program only lasted for four weeks. Where did the extra four weeks come from? How should those weeks be figured into the whole equation?

It felt so cold and contrived. Our hearts were deprived of the grace we craved. Instead the law template was laid out and traced. It hurt. We expected generous care and consideration; instead we received calculators and reluctantly doled out dictates. Ouch.

After reading Robynn's story, I felt torn. We have policies so that we use our resources wisely and are responsible in our use of time and yet we also need to show grace. Agencies must consider how leaders can show grace and follow policies at the same time. There were expectations to do things right; there were expectations for grace and understanding. Missionaries and their agency leaders are constantly working through such scenarios. There is always tension between caring for the person and pursuing organizational goals.

There are also other areas where a mission agency might be expecting more from a missionary than what she envisions. When a missionary joins a mission agency, she is thinking how to share the gospel with those who have yet to hear it. She is thinking of community development or medical missions. Her eye is on the goal of proclaiming Christ and making Him known. What she doesn't yet realize is that to do this, the mission agency expects her to put in time to send in the information it needs from her. She may be gifted at evangelism, but can she handle accounting? Foyle (1986) addresses what mission agencies sometimes erroneously expect from missionaries and how missionaries often feel ill-prepared for many of their roles:

> Missionaries often feel inadequately trained for their job, especially in areas of administration and personnel management, and brownout [*burnout*] may be precipitated by continued stress in those areas. This can be minimized by preliminary training, but unfortunately, missionaries are expected to know by instinct principles of group dynamics,

personnel management, accounting and bookkeeping, how to read a balance sheet and an audit, how to run meetings, and how to make a budget (p. 3).

Both the missionary and the mission agency ought to re-evaluate and communicate expectations. There are expectations from both sides and both need to be aware of what each expects. The returned surveys demonstrated that women have a wide range of feelings about their mission agencies from deep appreciation to extreme aggravation. Some women noted that their agencies exceeded their expectations and there were quite a few very positive comments, such as one woman who wrote, "They have met all of my expectations. I am very fortunate to work for an organization that truly takes care of their personnel overseas. I could not ask for any more." On the other hand, one woman wrote on her survey about her agency, "They gave the Holy Spirit the left foot of fellowship about three years ago. They seem to be more concerned with power plays than field ministry. I've learned not to have any expectations. I honestly don't care what they do." This was by far the harshest statement. Negative feelings this strong were extremely rare. Most women were more than satisfied with and were committed to their agencies, appreciated them and, though they recognized their agencies weren't perfect, were content with them and happy to be a part of them. They appreciated good health care, member care, retirement benefits, organizational structure and vacation policies. They felt that their relationship with their sending agencies was characterized by openness to communication and a concern for their well-being. Having conferences and times of interaction, maintaining communication and offering times of debriefing are valued.

In summary, missionary women must discuss their expectations and be assertive in communicating their ideas and concerns to mission leadership. They do not have to wait to be asked for their input, but need to volunteer for committees and to contribute to leadership as they want to and are able. Women can also talk with their direct supervisors about any issues they might have as well as seek out a more experienced woman missionary from whom they can get practical help and advice. Mission leadership must intentionally seek to know their women members, their gifting and abilities so they can utilize all personnel in fulfilling the great commission. They must communicate care and affirmation, recognizing the value women members bring to their organization. They can prepare women for their various roles in ministry within their homes and host communities by helping them form ministry plans with flexibility and freedom, as well as accountability. Mission leaders can encourage husbands to come alongside their wives in helping them. Leaders need to also encourage single women in their ministries while recognizing limitations and struggles they might also have. Leadership can show concern and care while following policies and using resources wisely. With these things as foundations, missionary women will stay more committed to their sending agencies and their calling. I feel great optimism for all that the missionary and the mission agency will do together for the glory of God, especially as they strive to clarify expectations of each other and show grace and forgiveness in the process.

Survival Tip #4
Endure with glorious power

In light of the seeming bureaucracy of sending center policy and the weight of the expectations we live under, whether real or perceived, it's easy to lose hope. It's easy to get bogged down in the forms, in the requirements. It's easy to feel undervalued, unappreciated and unknown or unloved. It's easy to give up!

God highly values perseverance. He puts so much stake in it that He puts all of His power behind it, to support it, to endorse it. Colossians 1:11 says,

> We also pray that you will be strengthened with all his glorious power so you have all the endurance and patience you need. (NLT)

All of the Power of God… all of His *glorious* power will strengthen you. For what? What would God dedicate all of His glorious power to? To what cause would He give all of His glorious power? He gives it so that you will be strengthened. Not strengthened to work harder, to entertain more guests, to lead more people to Christ. Not strengthened to lead more team meetings, to fill out more forms from headquarters. Strengthened so that you will have *all* the endurance and patience you need.

God so values endurance and patience, He's willing to donate all of His glorious power toward it!

But why to endurance? What does endurance accomplish? James 1: 2-4 reads,

Dear brothers and sisters, when troubles come your way, consider it an opportunity for great joy. For you know that when your faith is tested, your endurance has a chance to grow. So let it grow, for when your endurance is fully developed, you will be perfect and complete, needing nothing. (NLT)

Endurance results in our completion, our perfection. God is so completely committed to that! He wants to see us grow up. He longs for it. He's staked all of his glorious power behind it.

The other day while reading these verses I (Robynn) told God how annoyed I was that it was endurance that brings about my perfection, my completion. Why couldn't it be another virtue? Why not compassion? Or service? Endurance implies something to endure. The very word assumes sorrows to go through, suffering to embrace, tears to cry, disappointments to lament. To endure means to go through that and more. It hurts. There will be pain and often true agony. Endurance means accepting from God that which will make us perfect and complete.

How odd and amazing that He provides all of His glorious power to strengthen us for such a high calling—He strengthens us to endure!

FIVE

THE EXPLORATION CONTINUES, EXPECTATIONS AND THE SENDING CHURCH

When we were in the process of becoming missionaries, people in our home context idealized us; they saw us as models of commitment and inspiration. – Lois and Larry Dodds

Not only do missionaries have expectations of themselves, the church that sends them also has expectations of them. Those called into full-time ministry are sometimes put on pedestals by others due to their passion and desire to serve God. Missionaries are also perceived as spiritual since they are willing to leave the comfort of their home, families and worldly wealth to serve God in other countries far from home. The Dodds (1997) tell of being idealized by people in their home context as "models of commitment and inspiration" (p. 5). I remember visiting a church to speak as a missionary and being asked by a young girl to autograph her Bible. That didn't seem quite right to me since I didn't write it! Like her, I simply believed it and sought to obey it. Careful to clarify that not all individuals or all churches are like this, one survey respondent wrote of some pressures she felt by a few people:

Though not all individuals in our home churches feel this way, we have definitely been confronted through the years by well-respected church members and staff who have expressed [expectations] ... along these lines: to be superhuman/super spiritual, to have a large list of converts, to do nothing that costs a lot of money (on self or children), to never eat out at restaurants (when in the U.S. or abroad), to drive very old, broken-down vehicles and not complain, to not receive any paid vacation, to act like Mary, but be more like Martha."

Missionaries often leave for their field of service in the midst of fanfare. Supporters commit to pray for and give toward their ministry. Missionaries want to be faithful to their call and the church's mandate and to use these resources wisely. Most of the women surveyed indicated that they think their sending churches expect them to minister faithfully and effectively as well as to report back to the church what God is doing through them.

Some missionaries had leadership roles in their home countries and churches. They wielded influence over their congregations and communities. Jones (1995) points out the contrast in roles that the missionary experiences when first going abroad: viewed as leaders in their home country, they then move overseas where they are seen as learners studying language and culture. She explains that the influential leader turned missionary changes from the expert to the learner. This role shift may cause her to lose confidence in herself for a time. This change can be stressful for the missionary and may affect how she relates to her church, as well as potentially changing the church's perspective of her, if she is open and honest about some of her struggles.

Some missionary women, according to the survey, think that they are expected by their churches to thrive spiritually, but also are concerned they may be occasionally judged as unspiritual if they return home or suffer extreme discouragement or burnout. Perry (1982) writes that missionaries who burn out and leave ministry may be judged as weak, carnal, not walking with God or disobedient to the Lord. Burnout is sometimes equated with failure. Whether missionaries are coming or going, they believe the church has expectations of them. Whether these are real expectations or perceived ones, they aren't sure, however these expectations can feel very real.

Some churches have programs or a curriculum that missionaries go through in order to be sent out by the church. Most of these requirements are written out and focus on their preparation to go. It is clear to missionary men and women what they need to do if they want to be supported and sent out by the church. There is an excellent and thorough example of a missionary preparation program at Calvary Church in Lancaster, Pa. (www.calvarychurch.org)

Once missionaries are overseas, there are fewer guidelines for them from the church regarding expectations. Some churches want an annual review, but leave it to the mission agency to follow through on what is expected of missionaries once they are overseas. Churches and mission agencies can work together when issues arise for member care.

When asked what they thought their churches expected of them, some missionary women weren't sure. Most felt that they were expected to walk with God and serve Him faithfully. They felt supported and cared for by their churches. They felt they were expected to communicate regularly with their churches. Married missionary women with children felt like their supporting churches understood their "dual" roles as homemakers and missionaries and didn't expect more than they were able to produce in either area.

There has been an increase in missions education for churches. This has helped shape the church's expectations of the missionary. Churches seek to be more intentional about missions and more members have been on short-term missions trips. That, along with globalization and a keener understanding of different cultures, has given churches a greater understanding of missionaries, where they live and what they do.

We'll let some missionary women themselves tell you about their positive experiences with their supporting churches:

- They are very supportive–they want me to be real about my life here; [they] enjoy benefitting from insights I bring back or hearing about what I have learned along the way. They don't expect me to be super mum or super missionary, but want to facilitate me 'joining in with what God is doing' as far as possible.

- I really believe that they do not expect me to be perfect, to never fail, to never get tired, to never have culture shock, to never be homesick. I really believe they sent me as I am, as the Lord will work through me and my family.

- I must say that our home fellowship is much more clued into the 'real' world of my work than most places. They love us, care for us and don't expect us to speak 3,000 times or be present every single Sunday we are back in the States.

- They have been really great. Truthfully, I think they expect faithfulness on our part. They do not press us for numbers although they do like to hear from us with news updates and prayer requests. They have been an extraordinary support and prayer partners. Our missions pastor has visited us twice and his ministry to us really helped in some difficult times.

- We're really blessed to have a sending fellowship that does not pressure us to 'perform.' They support us greatly and probably mostly just expect that we'll communicate and ask them for needs and prayer and partner with them. I feel encouraged by our sending fellowship and they've been a great source of comfort when I've felt overwhelmed.

When missionaries are first sent out by their sending church, there is usually a strong relationship connecting them. In the beginning, people write to the missionary. As time goes on, church members are involved with family issues, church ministries and communicating with a missionary they don't often see falls last on the to-do list. Missionaries have come to know and expect that churches pray and appreciate it immensely, but also recognize that the church members don't necessarily write to let them know of it very often.

Over time some missionary women felt a gap developed between their passion for missions and the church's passion for missions. At times someone in a supporting church would come up to ask a missionary how her ministry is going and she may begin to tell of it. However, when the listener would seem to lose interest after two or three minutes, the missionary realizes she only needs to give a very short answer in order to satisfy the person's interest. One missionary woman wrote:

> I also thought people would love to hear about my experiences, but I find most people can listen for three to five minutes and that's about it, because they have no connection with you, no point of reference.

Of course, it must be asked how much effort the missionary woman puts into listening to members of her sending church tell about their lives! Building relationships takes both parties. It would seem active listening on both sides would be deeply appreciated.

Other missionary women wrote about what they thought their churches expected of them and we can extract from that a bit of what they expected from their churches:

🝊 Regular updates. There is little correspondence with our sending church. This has been hurtful, but is accepted as normal now. We update as we can and even call our pastor to see how we can pray for him. We understand that the dynamics at our church are changing and it is difficult for them to remember us as we are out of sight. I have no doubt that they do pray for us, just little correspondence.

🝊 When we went on furlough the first time, it seemed that everyone had their own lives and were content to give money without really wanting to know how we are. And so, in retrospect, I think churches expect a lot less of us than we assume."

We can see the missionary women expected more frequent communication as well as being thought of or remembered more often.

As time goes on, churches change. Some people leave and new people come. There may be a different pastor. People rotate on and off of the missions committee. The missionary comes home after a term overseas only to discover that they no longer know most of the people in the church. They begin to build new friendships if they are on furlough for a while near the church. They go back overseas and return home several years later, only to have the pattern repeated. Several women write about these changes and how they are affected by them:

🝊 My sending fellowship has changed so much that I really don't know what they think of me or expect from me … when we left, it was like family and I was a cherished member raised up by my church family and sent out. Now I don't know those in leadership very well.

Unfortunately, I think they expect me to have all of my needs met by my sending organization and do not think that I am personally accountable to them. I wish this weren't true, but I'm afraid there's not a strong connection with them. There's a whole new staff there since I left for the field and the congregation has grown from 500 to 2,500. I feel like I just get lost in the crowd when I'm there and most people don't know who I am. I realize that this is my fault and I definitely see things that I could have done differently over the years.

Sometimes I feel like they are just happy I'm going so they won't have to (when all the while I'm thankful I don't have to stay in America!). I think I fill a missions slot for them—a missions moment, a women's speaker, a table at a missions conference. I feel when I'm gone, they really don't think about me much, except for a few exceptional female prayer warriors who are real saints in my book because they love the lost. In some ways, I am thankful that they expect very little from me, because I am so stretched time-wise. In other ways, I feel sad that they are not interested in missions—it is just one program of many in a church or just delegated to a select few (like a hobby, almost!). For me, missions is an all-consuming fire; for them, it's interesting to think about during missions week.

I'm speaking in gross generalities, but you get the picture. Twenty years ago, pastors gave us the whole service to share about the work—even the special music time! This was [in] several different denominations, as we had friends from all walks of life. The time we have been given to share during a service has been whittled down over the years—15 minutes, five minutes and last time the church had us stand up and wave to the parishioners.

Again, the missionary has responsibilities to pursue relationships, to be in contact with church members and to take the initiative to build bridges with her supporting church. Simply because the church limits the time missionaries have to share in the service does not necessarily mean the church is losing her vision for missions. Missionaries may be asked to share more in Sunday school classes or small groups than in the main service. Both the church and the missionary need to be intentional in communicating with each other. The onus is not only on the church.

In being supported by the church, one missionary woman was afraid she was seen as a burden to others when she was home on furlough. Missionaries often need a place to stay, a vehicle, help to find doctors or babysitters. They are looking for opportunities to share their ministry and churches graciously invite them to speak, open their homes and share their cars and meals. Such generosity is overwhelming! Missionaries are thankful, but sometimes feel like they are always receiving and fear they might cause undue hardship for churches who give so much already. More often than not, these fears are unfounded. Churches who give and pray are excited and thankful to be apart of what God is doing around the world. Read what Robynn experienced when she had a need:

> We were expecting our third child. Here it was the middle of December, just a month before my due date. We learned that there was no way for my parents to come from Pakistan without jeopardizing their visas. The business Lowell was with had scheduled a language camp not only for Lowell to teach at, but also for us to host during the last week of January. Our best friends Donnie and Beth had a mandatory conference they needed to attend. They would be in town for the birth, but needed to leave soon after. Our team was either falling apart or away from town. One couple had left the previous summer. We were helping to sort out their belongings. Christmas outreach loomed large. We were hosting two particularly demanding

short-termers. And our water situation was horrendous. We had none. I had just hired plumbers and construction workers to build us our own water tank on the roof, instead of relying on the landlord's ancient pump. I was enormously pregnant.

In a moment of desperation, Lowell wrote a last minute email to our sending church in Kansas. He explained the situation we were in, and, apologizing for the last minute request, he asked for help. Could the church send someone to help us during the birth of our baby? Could someone come to help entertain four-year-old Connor and two-year-old Adelaide? Could someone come cook, clean and help juggle all the other domestic challenges? Could someone *please* come and help?

Within a couple of days our church got back to us. Two ladies were immediately chosen. Passports were expedited. Visas were applied for. Bronwynn was born on January 17. On January 22 our two angel friends, Yvonne and Susan, arrived. They jumped into our family and into our lives and were a tremendous blessing. They helped with three children, cooked meals and made tea. They helped us host the language camp—including looking after several additional children during that time. They were amazing.

We asked for help, knowing it was so last minute. The church's response was beyond our wildest expectations. What a blessing!

Not all churches are able to respond and provide the kind of support Robynn's church provided. Possibly not every missionary would ask. Much depends on the relationship between the missionary and the church. If the bond is strong or if there is a past record of the church coming to the rescue, missionaries may feel freer to ask for aid. But if there isn't a strong relationship or if the missionary is afraid to show such vulnerability then help will probably not be sought; because of this it is unable to be given. It would help if the church missions committee or contact person and the missionary could sit together at least once per term and talk about expectations, as well as the joys of giving and receiving in the Lord. Missionaries need the freedom to share their sorrows and their joys. I don't think churches expect missionaries to be perfect, but are their expectations realistic? Missionaries don't expect churches to meet their every need but what do they expect? Discussion together could only help. Could churches and missionaries come up with a contract or covenant which would state expectations on both sides? I'm sure other agencies have something similar, but Christar has a template of a covenant that can be adapted to fit with different churches' and missionaries' needs. It is dated and signed by the missionary, the sending church and the mission agency so that there is better understanding on the roles each partner plays:

Partnership Agreement Between Christar and Sending Church

Christar exists to glorify God by establishing churches among the least-reached Buddhists, Hindus, Muslims and other Asians worldwide.

Our Lord commanded us to make disciples of all nations. The biblical role of the local church is to send out missionaries. The role of the mission agency is to come alongside the church and facilitate this process. Christar and **Sending Church** agree to work together to fulfill the Great Commission. By working together, we believe that we can accomplish more for the glory of God than if we work separately. We agree to cooperate under the partnership terms outlined below:

1. **Appointee** will be sent out by **Sending Church** and

hold membership with Christar.

2. Christar will assign **Appointee** to a specific ministry in **Country**. This assignment will be consistent with the missionary calling of **Appointee** and the vision of **Sending Church**.

3. **Appointee** will be an integral part of a Christar team in **Country** and will be subject to the policies and direction of Christar. Christar and **Sending Church** will work together to ensure **Appointee's** faithfulness and fruitfulness in ministry. Ministry reports, goals and prayer letters will be available to both Christar and **Sending Church**.

4. The ultimate spiritual authority for **Appointee** resides with **Sending Church**. **Sending Church** delegates to Christar responsibility for pastoral care and direct supervision of **Appointee** during service on the field.

5. During home ministry, **Appointee** will be responsible to Christar. However, **Appointee** will have significant interaction with **Sending Church** during home ministry. Christar and **Appointee** will give consideration to the need for additional training during home ministry, as deemed necessary.

6. If personal or family difficulties arise for **Appointee**, Christar and **Sending Church** will work together to provide appropriate care, including biblical counseling, if warranted.

7. This agreement is in effect from **Date Appointed** until the termination of **Appointee's** ministry with Christar, in accordance with Christar bylaws and policies, or

through mutual agreement between Christar and **Sending Church**.

In wanting to support missionaries and projects that are meaningful and fruitful, churches rightfully want to know that their support is being invested wisely. However, missionaries may be afraid of losing support if they share some of their more difficult struggles. If they only share triumphs, then it is no wonder churches might tend to have higher expectations of them. If they share only struggles, why would the church want to invest in perceived failure? Finding the right balance, sharing the good and the bad, is helpful for the missionary and the church. Also, it may be helpful for the church to find the right balance in asking for results and being aware of the missionary, her circumstances and the resistance of the area where she is ministering.

The missionary woman would like to have, and starts out expecting to have, a strong and close relationship with her home church family. According to the survey, 50 percent of missionary women had higher expectations for staying connected and having a strong relationship with their sending church than what they were experiencing. This tells us that half of the women missionaries surveyed would like a deeper, stronger relationship with their supporters. One woman expressed her disappointment in her home church, writing, "I wish they would show more interest. I feel like I'm stuck in a loveless marriage." She wanted a closer relationship and desired for them to show more of an interest in her and her ministry. I'm sure she had a responsibility for her own communication with the church. It is clear, though, that she felt a disconnect between herself and her church.

By far, the survey indicated that missionary women were extremely thankful for their church's support and understanding. They felt loved and supported. Their relationship with their sending church is critical to them. They treasure the relationships they've formed and miss them when they wane. How thankful we are for those who give, who pray and send so that those who've never heard the gospel and are not a part of the kingdom of God have the opportunity to join the body of Christ. One day we will all gather around the throne to worship the King of Kings and Lord of Lords: those who sent missionaries, the missionaries and those who responded to the gospel message. We will all stand amazed at the grace of God in allowing us to come into His presence and spend eternity with Him. Only then will we see the full strategic influence of those who have prayed and sacrificially given so that the gospel could go to those who needed to hear it. With eternity in view, may churches continue to pray, give and send out missionaries; may missionaries be faithful to their call and the mandate of the church; and may the Savior of the world be praised.

Survival Tip #5
Recognize the love God has for his bride

During our second furlough, a profound thought struck me: God loves the Bride of Christ! This is a basic elementary thought. God loves the Church. He is preparing her especially for His beloved Son. He is grooming her and clothing her and seeing to all the arrangements for this glorious union. Nothing gives Him greater joy.

I went to South Asia with a passion to see the Bride of Christ there. And I fell in love with her, too. I loved worshipping in Hindi. I loved the forms that believers there had adopted to articulate and express their faith. It was a beautiful and thrilling thing: the Bride dressed in a glittering red sari with sequins and embroidery work, with an elaborate woven gold border. I could see her jewelry and the intricate henna designs on her hands and up her arms. She is glorious.

Return culture shock blurred my vision and it wasn't always so easy to be thrilled about the Bride of Christ in North America when we came back. I found that I was critical and judgmental. Particularly when we live under the weight the expectations our sending church may have for us, whether those are real or imaginary, we may become defensive and on edge. Our own expectations to be heard, to be cared for, to be accepted and enthusiastically supported take precedence in our minds. We become self-obsessed and cynical. This is not good.

It's time to remember that elementary truth: God loves the Bride of Christ. He is just as thrilled about her, in spite of her imperfections, in your sending country as in the country you are called to. Her radiance glows whether she's wearing a red kimono with long flowing sleeves or a white dress with a veil over her face. As she anticipates her Groom, as she readies for His return, her excitement is contagious. Others see her and they want to join the party. God the Father sees her and He marvels that His Son gets to be the Groom! He loves the Bride of Christ. We have the privilege of serving and loving the Bride as well.

SIX

THE EXPLORATION CONTINUES, EXPECTATIONS AND CO-WORKERS

Missionary women tend to be more tuned in and critical of how other missionary women spend their time. –N. Crawford

I am thankful for the friendships I have with women who were on my team in the Middle East. These relationships run deep. We have seen each other at some of our weakest moments; we have prayed for each other and worked alongside each other; we have seen God work through our weaknesses with His strength. Not every one was a "best friend," but we were committed to each other and to our shared ministry. I don't remember expecting to have a best friend on my team, but I did expect good relationships.

Women in the survey had some expectation of having a best friend on their team. Half of those surveyed had higher expectations in this area than what they were experiencing, whereas 20 percent were having better relationships than what they thought they would. When asked about her expectation of having a strong team, 50 percent were disappointed and 35 percent were experiencing what they had expected. This means that even during training and orientation before going overseas, when they hear about team dynamics and challenges, half of the women still have some expectation that they will have a best friend on their pretty strong team.

One contributing factor is that missionaries may arrive overseas better prepared to work among national friends than to work with each other; that is, they may receive more orientation regarding relating to national friends and culture than to teammates and team culture. While they tend to tolerate a degree of disappointment with their unsaved national friends, missionaries look at each other and tend to expect certain behavior from each other as co-workers. There is also pressure to conform to these expectations. Chester (1983) portrays what missionaries themselves seem to be thinking: "Though I'm under a lot of stress I cannot let the others know. I don't understand why they look so calm and seem to not be under much stress. I must keep up my front of calmness" (p. 35). Some missionaries may feel it is not appropriate to express anger or other emotions that could be perceived negatively by others on their team. They fear being viewed as unspiritual. Team members definitely have expectations of each other. One woman, due to a change in her circumstances, wrote about her struggle to do or be what she thought her team expected of her:

> When I started in cross-cultural work I was married, but didn't have children. I was able to work alongside my husband and be very involved in our church-planting team ministry. Since that time, though, we've had two children and my role as a mother is taking a high priority in my life. Because of that, I can't do everything/be everything that I thought I could or that I think people expect me to do/be. That has been and continues to be a challenge, as I learn how to still be involved, but put my family first. Sometimes it is hard to block out other people's comments on how they think you should or should not be involved.

Team members expect involvement from all team members, including wives and mothers (Hawkins, 1994). Commenting particularly about teammates' expectations of women, Hawkins, in exploring expectations of married missionary women specifically writes, "Her coworkers expect her to attend all the team meetings. They feel that she needs to be involved in all the activities. She must also do her fair share of teaching children and ladies' Bible classes. Resources and personnel are limited. Everyone needs to participate" (p. 1). Crawford (2005) acknowledges this pressure from other missionaries for women and cited an example of one woman who was hurt by others' critical judgment. This missionary mother tried to balance her ministry in her home and outside of the home; however, no matter how hard she tried to fill both roles, she felt criticized by other missionaries. Her experience illustrates how missionary mothers feel the quandary of balancing ministry to their children with ministry to national friends. Women also deal with being judged by others as to how they are doing balancing their roles in the community and in their homes. One woman wrote on the survey:

> Team work is harder than I imagined–but very fulfilling and rewarding, too. I have enjoyed the interaction and friendship. Sometimes, the interaction and expectations are too high–I can feel squeezed at times and unnecessarily burdened by their expectations and requests. Balancing those needs has been a challenge, but worth it.

Another missionary mentioned that she noticed how tough we can be on each other. So, not only do missionary women feel expectations from other missionaries, there can be a sense of competition. Who is ministering more? Whose gifts seem most important? One missionary woman expressed her surprise that she had become so judgmental of others. Unfortunately, she is not alone. Crawford (2005) notes that missionary women themselves are often the harshest critics of other missionary women and how they spend their time. A missionary woman described this

very thing when wrote on the survey that other missionaries'
expectations of her made her feel like giving up:

> What makes me feel like giving up? 'Other missionaries'
> expectations of me as a woman ... that I should be a 'stay-at-
> home' mother and wife and not have my own role ... there
> are certain people who always bring it up ... they are mostly
> other women!"

I confess that at times I have looked at other women and made
judgments that I had no business making. I am ashamed to say
that though I may not have judged others verbally, my heart was
not right. It is probable that others wondered about me and my
use of time as well. One of my former teammates who is married
with children now but was single when she was on my team told
me she was sorry if she ever gave me the impression that I wasn't
working hard enough. She now had more appreciation for what
I was going through because she is experiencing it herself. I never
felt judged by this dear friend, only encouraged. However, I think
she must have wondered a little bit about my work ethic since she
thought enough about it to say something to me.

I am very thankful that it is not others' judgment that counts.
God is our only judge and the only one whose opinion matters. It
is not other people's expectations or opinions that will matter in
the end. We need to encourage each other and spur one another
on. There may be a time when it is appropriate to gently and
lovingly challenge one another. However, we should not judge
harshly or hold people to our own personal standards and goals.
We are in the body of Christ to complete, not compete.

Newer missionaries expect much from more experienced
missionaries. They inadvertently expect them to be spiritually mature,
loving and godly simply because they are missionaries who are serving
God (Dodds, 1997). The Dodds emphasize these high expectations
and the ensuing disappointment in the following example:

An especially gifted young missionary in Nepal was overtly persecuted by an older missionary, jealous for her husband's position. How does one reconcile such an experience with the pedestal ideal which fills the literature and training programs? (p. 13)

Women in the surveys also share some of their unmet expectations by their team:

- Team members had different expectations for me than I had for myself.

- When we arrived our coworkers were established and busy so did not interact with us much. We were left to figure out life for ourselves. Sadly, when new people have come out I have been too busy to interact or mentor them.

- The expectations about the job itself were met. My role as a team member has been the most difficult to work through. I expected a unified, harmonious body focused on accomplishing the same task/vision of reaching others for Christ. It was shocking to hear quarrels over strategies, budgets, projects. I expected missionaries to be spiritual leaders, not consumed with earthly desires.

It must also be mentioned that some experienced missionaries may feel that the newer missionaries may be expecting too much from them. They may come asking for a mentor, looking for direction, needing more than a leader is able to give. The more experienced missionary may expect the newer one to do more on their own before they feel ready. These unfulfilled expectations hurt the newer missionary and drain the more experienced one; the relationship is fractured as no one's expectations are being met.

Newer missionaries also tend to have high expectations of those in missions whom they have heard about, possibly read books by and about and perhaps whom God has used to draw them to missionary service. These high expectations based on famous missionaries or missionary stories lead to a "professional mystique,"—an unrealistically high expectation based on image more than reality and a critical issue relevant to expectations and burnout for missionaries.

The problem of basing one's expectations on professional mystique has been described by Perry (1982) as "patterning one's life after another person or a certain image of a profession, and later becoming disillusioned with that person and/or profession" (p. 46). Many young people read missionary biographies. In the book, *Dorothy Carey, The Tragic and Untold Story of Mrs. William Carey*, author James R. Beck noted that the biographers of William Carey portrayed him as never discouraged and never complaining. Beck points out that this cannot be true based on Carey's own journal. Carey wrote of himself, "I don't love to be always complaining–yet I always complain." In portraying missionaries as nearly faultless, writers do future missionaries a disservice. Biographies and books need to describe the realities of missions, not just successes and seeming perfection. In a 2002 letter from George Verwer about why missionaries leave the field, he affirms the need to write realistic books about missions, "As a book pusher I must confess that it often is books that create this unrealistic expectation. We have too many books with nice formulae and not enough with honesty, balance and biblical reality."

Future missionaries also listen to missionary speakers who share what God is doing through them and others around the world. Some of these stories are amazing; however, as mentioned earlier in the book, if stories of failure, sorrow and the mundane are left out, listeners do not get a full picture of what missionary life is like. This can add to professional mystique as it presents an unrealistic picture of what missions and missionaries are like. When new missionaries blinded by professional mystique arrive on the field, their eyes are opened to the reality that those whom God uses are sinners saved by His amazing grace, but still sinners. Every missionary faces hardship, discouragement and failures. Every missionary should be sharing some of those stories as well as the ones where there is great or small success. Potential missionaries need to hear about language mistakes, getting lost and lapses of electricity, and not just souls being won and churches being planted. Missionary life includes all of the above and new missionaries would be better prepared for team life and missions because they would come with more realistic expectations of themselves and others.

Sometimes newer missionaries may not expect help to be available (Jaffe, 1984). If, in fact, assistance is available, failing to seek it out and utilize it can contribute to burnout. If a missionary arrives on the field not expecting help from anyone, she may act aloof and seem able to handle it all on her own. Other missionaries get the idea that she does not want or need any help, so her expectation comes true and she is not aided by others. I was once confronted by a co-worker about not caring enough to help her. I was surprised; I thought the woman was doing very well and did not need any help from others. She had come across as self-reliant and had not openly shared her needs. This hurtful miscommunication illustrates what can happen when help is neither offered nor asked for.

I also remember thinking I should be able to "do it all" without any help from others as a newly arrived missionary. I couldn't keep up with the home. I was trying to put in language study hours. I tried harder and harder, and grew more and more frustrated and tired. I wanted to be like the missionary women whose biographies I had read. This chaos did not last long, however. I went out to dinner with my husband and shared everything that was on my discouraged and overwhelmed heart.

Thanks to a responsive husband and to women who responded when I admitted I needed help and came alongside me to help, I didn't give up or burn out.

Expectations, whether of the new missionary or of the more experienced one, affect team dynamics. It has been said in missionary circles that the primary reason missionaries leave the field is interpersonal relationship problems with other missionaries. So it is worthwhile to ask, "How many of these problems are caused by unmet, unstated and possibly unrecognized expectations?" Missionaries usually arrive on the field more prepared to deal with issues that arise in a new culture and with national friends than they are with interpersonal relationships at a team level.

Based on comments from the survey, women have experienced some great team relationships and some not so great ones. There is nothing like a team setting for developing either deep and life-long relationships or dire and lasting divisiveness. Communicating expectations, forgiving when disappointed and showing gratitude when expectations are met all build into team dynamics. Teammates who can be real with each other and not try to keep wearing their missionary masks will bond more and serve more dynamically than those who try to portray spirituality to the detriment of themselves and others. Let some of the women who responded to the survey share some of the surprises they experienced on their teams:

The biggest thing that impressed me right off was how everyone shares stuff—like we're one big family. I'd never think of asking my neighbors/friends in the states if I could borrow stuff like I do here! I really like that. We've been blessed to be around teams that put a big emphasis on us all being family—I love being an aunt to other people's kids. We just have so many really great people that we get to work with. It amazes me.

◑ There are certain traits that tend to make for successful missionaries–self-motivation, self-discipline, the ability to 'fly by the seat of your pants,' a certain fearlessness and 'depart from the mold' personality. Those very traits, however, often make it difficult for those types of personalities to work together. It has been a surprise to see the extent to which cross-cultural workers don't get (along) with one another, nor do they really trust one another.

◑ It surprised me that the teams I have been with and the team I am working with have become such a great support and encouragement to me that I never thought it could be so important for me. It surprised me that [in] working with other cross-cultural workers, [we] need to put a lot of time in the beginning to build trust and understanding, but after we know how to relate and work with one another (teammates from different cultural backgrounds), it is a great joy to experience the kind of team life (like a family) that the Lord desires.

◑ It seems that strengths become magnified in cross-cultural work, but then so do weaknesses, and often we did not even realize that those weaknesses existed. So sometimes team members are going through stresses brought on as a result of the cross-cultural experience and other team members may experience the backlash. Not always pleasant or fun. On the other hand, I do not believe that I would have ever worked anywhere in the U.S. that I would have developed the personal and working relationships that I have with my team members. I love them dearly and they love me and I know that they would support me through whatever, as I would for them. They have, in effect, become my family on the field. Sometimes we are dysfunctional, but it seems to me that there is always love involved.

🔾 Team life is hard, but very refining. It's like marriage. It's like family. You love each other (at least after a while). You heartily disagree. You get mad at each other and work things out. You suffer together. You live in close community, seeing each other a lot. It's the hardest thing and the best thing.

🔾 [I'm surprised by] ... our ability to sin as badly as anyone else and to be harder to get along with than ordinary church members; our spiritual immaturity in dealing with conflict between team members ...

Team life is about relationships and opportunities for trust or disappointment abound. People are stretched and need each other. We look to each other for guidance, goal setting and taking care of each other. Robynn has a story about a yellow flat that shows her expectations as a newcomer trying to trust her teammate when choosing a place to live:

It was such a perfect flat. There were three bedrooms, three bathrooms, a large central dining room, a sitting room and a wonderfully, surprisingly modern kitchen. One of the bedrooms was tiny and could have made the perfect office. It was a new house and had been newly painted a lovely shade of pale yellow. What made the place perfect was it had a back garden accessed through a screen door off the dining area. From there you could see the glorious Ganges River.

We had looked for an apartment for over three and a half weeks. We had scoured the neighborhood Lowell had previously lived in. Nothing was suitable. Looking slightly further a field was also fruitless. We could not find a place to live. Meanwhile, we stayed with our team leaders James and Dina and their two little girls in their small upstairs apartment. As accommodating and hospitable as they were, we knew we had outstayed our welcome. They needed their family space back to themselves.

When we happened upon the yellow apartment through a servant of a friend of a friend it seemed too good to be true. The landlord was asking Rs 3200 a month for it. James thought that was too much. He was confident that he could talk the landlord down to a more reasonable amount. Lowell and James set off one evening to negotiate the details for our new home! I was so excited. As they left I prayed. And I moved in. I set up the kitchen in my mind. I imagined fixing sweet little meals there for my husband. I imagined making up guest beds for imaginary guests, showing them the bathroom, telling them to make themselves at home.

After a couple of hours Lowell and James returned. The landlord would not agree to anything less than his asking amount. He was set on Rs 3200 a month. James was adamant that this was too much. Lowell differed to James' experience and wisdom. The two of them walked away from the yellow apartment. I was devastated. I had just moved in! How could they do this to me? Rs 3200 was only $80! We could surely afford that. But apparently it wasn't the amount; it was the principle of the thing.

With tears in my eyes, I stopped cooking, I packed up the kitchen again, I stripped the guest beds, closed the door and walked away. I was angry and disappointed with Lowell, with James and with God.

Anyone who has ever been on a team can relate to the disappointment of decisions made that we don't necessarily agree with, but we go along with for the sake of unity or because we trust that the person with the most experience knows more than we do. People who have not been a part of a team may find this hard to understand. In our home country, we can probably decide where to live, what church to go to, how to spend our time. Within a team, much of this may be decided together. When there are few or no other believers in the country, we cannot church hop or find another supportive group of friends. The team is a lot of relationships all rolled into one group. Team life is not easy, even when expectations are recognized and communicated. If unspoken and unmet expectations are added to a team, with its various personalities and backgrounds, team life becomes even more difficult. When team life is difficult and a person is feeling alone or too harshly judged, an unhealthy response may lead to burnout. She may not have the emotional support she needs, the physical help she could use or the mental health to continue on in ministry healthily. As her energy wanes, she becomes more susceptible to burnout.

Before a new person arrives on the field, it would be wise for them to contact their future team and share some of their expectations. The team should then respond, clarifying what expectations may be easy to meet and where there might be challenges. The team could take the initiative and also share what they normally expect from a new team member. In Christar we have a covenant that we read with candidates as they become appointees. On the one hand, new missionaries read what their commitment is to us and to the Lord and then members respond with our commitment to them and to the Lord. It then might take them several months, if not years to arrive on the field. It might be wise for teams to have their own "covenant" for new team members covering what is expected of them and what they can expect from their new team.

Some newcomers would thrive on adventure and would love a "sink or swim" approach. They would love to arrive on the field and look for their own apartment or live with a national family.

They'd go out on their own, anxious for any new escapades and daring feats. Speaking as someone who was pushed off a dock as a little girl to sink or swim, and who didn't swim but quickly sunk (I'm only here because my sister pulled me out of the lake by my hair; thank you Debbie), there are those of us who need more care. Sometimes teams will walk with them, help them find an apartment or grocery shop. I remember calling our team leaders with questions and their availability to help. Much depends on who the team leaders are and what they are like as well. How important it is for team members to get to know future teammates before they arrive and to start building a relationship with them. Any information they can get on personality, likes and dislikes will be helpful for everyone's adjustment to team life. Proactive, regular communication between the field and the newcomer, especially about expectations, before the arrival date is essential.

As teams become more multicultural, there will need to be more discussion about expectations and how to communicate about them. We often go more prepared to understand our host culture than we are to understand the differing cultures of our teammates. Even if everyone is from the same culture, there are misunderstandings. With people on a team from different cultures holding varying degrees of expectations of what a team is, there must be more proactive discussions about team life. *Cross-Cultural Servanthood* by Duane Elmer as well as *Foreign to Familiar* by Sarah Lanier are excellent resources for team members to read together, to help us understand each other better as well as the cultures where we serve.

As team members work to recognize and communicate expectations, team life will go more smoothly and individuals on that team are more likely to thrive. When love is given and acceptance is expected, the foundation for trust is laid and the right to be heard is earned. In such an environment, team life still isn't easy, but it is a lot less difficult.

Survival Tip #6
Recognize the spiritual warfare

If there is one area that Satan would love to destroy it is this area of team relationships. This is the Body of Christ and he is deeply opposed to us. Interestingly a closer look at the famous spiritual warfare chapter, Ephesians chapter six, shows Paul examining different relational areas of conflict. He highlights husbands and wives, children and parents, employers and employees. And then he goes on to emphasize that our enemy is not a human being, our real enemy isn't that spouse, those kids, unsympathetic parents, nor is it your boss or your belligerent worker. Our real enemy is not, "flesh and blood," but rather is, "evil rulers and authorities of the unseen world ... mighty powers in this dark world, and ... evil spirits in the heavenly places" (Eph 6:12 NLT)

One night after we (Lowell and Robynn) had been in our new city for only five weeks, and while we were still living with our team leaders, we had an unusual experience. It was a Thursday. The team meeting was over, supper was cleared away, James and Dina had put the little girls to bed and were in their own room. Lowell and I were in bed ourselves debriefing the day. Suddenly and without pin-pointable cause I became very critical of each person on the team. I started in on a diatribe of negative observations. It was horrible and uncalled for. Soon after that a tremendous wave of fear took hold of me. I could feel it almost physically wash me over from my feet to my head. I clung to Lowell and began to cry. I told him I was afraid and that we should go home—back to North America. When I opened my eyes there was a strange sight above my head. I blinked repeatedly but the visitation did not end. Floating above us were several heads, almost like dark-colored balloons. They were jeering and laughing at us, at me in particular. Lowell immediately told me to pray but I was paralyzed spiritually. He then led me through a prayer and I repeated the phrases he said. Lowell then prayed over us both. As soon as he commanded the enemy to leave the room, our teammate's daughter, Anna began to cry out. Lowell and I got up and went to wake James and Dina. Sure enough Anna had thrown up. We told them what had happened and we helped to clean up Anna and resettle her. Afterwards the four of us prayed through the entire house. Lowell and I sat up and prayed and sang praise songs for awhile before going to sleep. The skirmish was over. Of course, we were on the winning side. The next morning God did a sweet thing. Normally the little girls woke up very early, usually around five o'clock. However that next morning the whole household slept until eight in the morning. It was a sweet peaceful sleep that the Father graced us with.

Nearly three years later I wrote a prayer letter with the following story in it:

> ...I heard our son (six month old) Connor crying in the night. I stumbled into his room and sat quietly on the guest bed listening to see whether or not he'd go back to sleep. As I was waiting I hummed the lullaby I had sung to him hours earlier in putting him to sleep, "All night, all day, Angels watching over me, my Lord." I looked up at his crib and saw four angels lounging around our sleeping son. A smile spread over my face. I couldn't stop the joy.

> "You don't need to worry, we're looking after him," the one nearest me said. Two sat on the side nearest the window, the other two on the door side. They were so relaxed and casual somehow. All of them were broad and big and bright and clean

cut! Suddenly I felt like I was intruding.

"Is it okay if I just sit here awhile?"

"Sure, you're welcome to," the nearest one reassured me.

"Should I cover him?"

"You can if you like, or we could take care of that for you."

"Thank you." With that I looked one last time at our four house guests and went back to bed still smiling profusely. I could hear the sweet sounds of Connor sucking his thumb.

God has looked after us on busy nights with overt demonic activity and on the quiet nights where the angels 'hung out' by the crib of a resting baby boy....

Never forget that the Great Commission Enterprise is a spiritual battle. Our enemy opposes what we do; he loathes us because of who loves us. He is threatened because he secretly knows that he has already lost! The Victory of Jesus was secured at the Cross and further cemented at the Resurrection. Never forget that! Keep reminding the unseen world that you remember that, and you remember it well!

There are countless wonderful books now out on spiritual warfare. There are hundreds of prayers you can pray renouncing Satan and all his forces daily. However there is no magical power in any of these prayers. God is the Protector. We pray to him. The power is His; it is not in the poetry of the words we say. It is not a complicated prayer to pray. You don't have to be in the Spiritual Special Forces to pray these prayers. Simply come to God as you already do and say,

"Father God I belong to you! Please remind Satan and his cohorts that I am yours and that you paid a high price to adopt me as your child. Remind the entire unseen world that Satan has no place in my life nor in my circumstances and that he has no authority over me. I belong to you the Most High God, the King of Heaven and earth, the Lord of Lords, the Great God of the universe. I belong to you and I am safe. Please protect me and my family and home from the attempts of the enemy to thwart your purposes in my life. In the holy name of Jesus, Amen."

SEVEN

THE EXPLORATION CONTINUES, EXPECTATIONS OF AND FOR HER HOST CULTURE

Your first term, you are likely to come at it from one extreme or another, either making little effort to accommodate the local culture for fear it isn't godly or that you won't be able to survive, or giving up everything you know and becoming a slave to local expectations.
– Marti Smith

As believers in our home cultures we need to live biblically; the challenge is figuring out how to do that since Christians apply biblical principles differently. When we move to another culture, we not only have to differentiate between our home culture and host culture, we also need seek to live biblically, as followers of Christ in our new and different world. In our apartment we had a building caretaker. His wife would come up to help me clean and would bring her two little boys. They would play with our two sons. One of my friends, from a "higher" class, asked me one day how could I let our children play with the children of the caretaker. I responded that God loves us all, but I began wondering if I should not allow them to play with these children so that culturally I could build a stronger bridge to relate to this friend. As I contemplated this, the Holy Spirit reminded me of God's love for the poor, how He has no favorites and the evil of showing bias to anyone. I determined that, based on biblical teaching, I would continue to allow my children to play with the caretaker's children. Days later this same friend remarked to me that what impressed her most about me was my love for all people, and I was able to model and therefore explain to her more powerfully the love that God has for all of us and that He has no favorites. We have to share His love with everyone.

Sometimes we adapt to our new culture; sometimes we don't. Not every missionary adapts the same way or to the same extent. Trying to figure out what our new culture expects from us and what we are expecting from our new culture is not always easy. It is ironic that as missionaries, we seek to make our home in a new culture; we adapt, work hard and persevere. We may never feel totally at home or fit in completely, but we are comfortable and our national friends become comfortable with us. When it is time to return to our home country, we may find that we really no longer fit in there either. We expect to; after all, it is our home. But we have changed. Our culture has undergone some changes as well and we weren't there to be a part of those changes. The disadvantage of this is that though we may feel comfortable both places, we never really, totally fit anywhere again. The advantage is we have a clearer idea of what it means to be a citizen of heaven, that this earth is not our home.

However, while we are here we want to serve him effectively cross-culturally. Brent Lindquist in *Too Valuable to Lose* writes, "...missionaries report that they went overseas with expectations that were unrealistic with regard to being accepted in the culture, being able to minister, and understanding what the place of service would be like" (p. 244). Orientation and experience can help. The goal is to learn and develop as a missionary in our new culture before the stress of dealing with unrealistic expectations leads to burnout.

Once a missionary arrives overseas, she becomes a part of a brand new culture with different role expectations for her. Dodds

(1997) discusses how difficult it is to enter a new culture and how missionaries can be criticized by nationals because they do not measure up to what is expected in their new situation. They are expected to take on the new, and in doing so it is easy for them to lose a bit of themselves. There is a certain loss of emotional balance as missionaries take on actions and words that are foreign. No amount of training can eliminate surprises and culture stress. Even though women may enter a new culture with a mental understanding that there will be culture stress and difficulties, the reality is usually worse than expected as new missionaries try to fit in and master the cultural dos and don'ts, often learning through their own mistakes.

Not only must a new missionary cope with the emotional stress or the spiritual stress of living in and adapting to a new culture, but she may also have to deal with these stresses while physically ill or weakened from exposure to unfamiliar sicknesses. I've heard some missionary women say they feel like they almost change personalities when they are overseas and sometimes it is hard to find their real selves again.

There is a relationship between expectations and performance when a person is adapting to a new culture (Jones, 1995). Sometimes a missionary's achievements increase because she tries harder to meet new expectations; but more often than not, achievements decrease because a new missionary cannot measure up to her own personal expectations to adapt. She grows tired of the inner conflict between her effort to achieve in her new culture compared to the perceivably inadequate results her efforts produce. Personal boundaries are pushed to the limit in order to succeed. If there is a desire to succeed in every area at all costs, burnout is a distinct possibility.

In seeking to adapt to a new culture, all missionary women deal with culture stress. Part of that stress is figuring out our roles. Based on the survey, 45 percent of the women said they thought they should be more certain of their roles and able to do them all well. That is hard to do when even figuring out what those roles are in a new culture is difficult. Hall cites Marjory Foyle, who wrote that married women might tend to struggle more than single women in expectations of her role:

> Single women working in cultures that hold very traditional views of women may find it easier to adapt to the situation than married women. Their singleness is an anomaly, and consequently they are considered social enigmas. In contrast, she suggests that married women have very strong role expectations imposed on them. (p. 306)

So single women, because they are thought of as unusual in some cultures, can sometimes operate outside of cultural expectations of her role, whereas married women may have to grapple with cultural expectations. For married women, if the role of a wife in her new culture is similar to the role she embraced in her home culture, there might be few difficulties. But if her new role is quite different, there will be more stress. For example a career-oriented wife might have difficulty making the adjustment to a culture where being a homemaker is more highly valued. In some countries it is part of her spiritual duty to have a clean house. If her house is dirty she may be judged as unspiritual. This adds to the pressure of upholding her role in the community as a godly wife and mother. She may need to adapt or work out how she fulfills her different roles in the community.

However, though single women might have more flexibility in their role as a single, they have their own struggles that married women do not have. There are constant questions about why the single missionary is not married, along with faulty assumptions as to the reason for her singleness; she may have to deal with frequent matchmaking attempts. Many conservative societies require a single woman to be careful of her reputation and to voluntarily give up many of the freedoms she enjoyed in her home culture, such as staying out after dark or associating with male friends. A single missionary will probably receive several marriage proposals and possibly more immoral propositions. The single missionary may have a harder time fitting into societies where marriage is highly valued. On the other hand, I have also observed situations in which my single friends were brought into families and found protection in their connections, as well as more open doors for ministry through those relationships than I, as a married woman, could ever have.

Hall (2003) agrees that there are complications regarding roles for women overseas when she notes that role expectations can be complicated for women missionaries, either expanding or limiting their activities. Living in a different culture with its own expectations of foreigners and trying to discern what their roles are in that culture can make a missionary woman's life challenging. Because of these role discrepancies and expectations in cross-cultural ministry, Crawford (2005) hones in on the importance of preparation and training for women, "One factor potentially mitigating the impact of host-culture gender-role expectations upon a female missionary's well-being may be the preparation of female missionaries to expect a discrepancy between their role and the expectations of the surrounding culture" (p. 196). The need for training women for these role complications cannot be overstated.

Especially in the beginning, it is hard for missionaries to know what the culture expects of them when they are trying to learn the language. Missionaries cannot just focus on language learning; they are also learning a totally new culture. Robynn found language and culture were intertwined as she approached the birth of her first child in her host culture:

> Our first child's birth was imminent. I was huge and awkward. I no longer risked wearing a sari, for fear I wouldn't balance it properly on the bump and it would fall off. I spent most of those last days close to our apartment.

I think it was the press wallah[1] who first asked about the *chinha*. After the baby was born would he get his *chinha*? What is *chinha*? *Chinha* is what you give me after the baby is born. I shrugged and assured him he'd get his *chinha*.

The post man wanted to know when he would be getting his *chinha*. I asked him what *chinha* was. He explained it was what I would give him after the baby was born. A tip? I inquired. No, not a tip. *Chinha*. Oh, I said. I shrugged and assured him he would be getting his *chinha*.

Our house helper Rama wanted to know if she'd be getting her *chinha*. I gave up asking what it was. It was something I'd give after the baby was born, that much I had managed to understand. I assured her she would be getting her *chinha*.

The tailor asked; the gas man asked; the subzi wallah[2] also asked.

When the press wallah came again and asked again I decided I really had to figure out what was expected of me. What on earth was *chinha*? After we reestablished that *chinha* was not a tip, and it wasn't sweets either, the press wallah went on to explain. *Chinha* was a sign. It was some*thing* I gave that whenever he would see it he would remember our child and be happy with us, something like a TV, or a radio, or a watch, or a wall clock—something that would remind him of our child and bring him joy. I asked whether just seeing the child wouldn't serve as a *chinha* of sorts. Oh no … that would never do. A *chinha* was something I gave after the baby was born … ya, ya, I got it!

---

1   The man who did our ironing
2   The vegetable seller

After that I stopped assuring people they would get their *chinha*. I asked my landlady about it. When the baby was born we gave sweets all around. We gave our house helper a new sari. We gave the press wallah a plate and told him to enjoy his *chinha* and the memories of our son.

The missionary woman goes overseas with high expectations regarding the degree to which she will embrace her new culture. Of the women who responded to the survey, 51 percent had higher expectations of embracing the culture than what they actually were experiencing. It is easy to go ready to adapt, cook, speak and act like our new friends. In reality it is a lot harder once you get there than the way it sounded during training.

Similarly, missionary women often feel they have a lot to offer. Frequently respected and loved in their home culture, missionary women may go into their host countries thinking that the new culture will be glad to have them. God has called them to go and serve Him in this new country. They expect that their new culture will gladly welcome them into their community. One woman, in response to the survey, wrote about her expectation to be warmly received:

> I unknowingly had this expectation that the nationals would be glad that we came! Ha! Not only do most of them not care, many would just as soon we leave. Don't get me wrong–I have some wonderful friends, but it's not like people are just sitting here waiting for workers to get off the plane and help them out. You really have to work to find a place in the community. Everything takes much, much longer than I anticipated– language learning, cultural learning, relationships ...

A key word here is this response is "unknowingly." This missionary's expectation did not become known until it was not met. I cannot stress enough the importance of thinking through what our expectations are when we go to serve cross-culturally. We need to ask ourselves, "What am I expecting when I arrive? What do I think the local culture will be like? How do I think they will respond to me?" Reading about our host culture is vital, as is recognizing what we are thinking and expecting as we study it. If I read that people are hospitable, do I expect to be invited to someone's home immediately? What do I think hospitality is like and how would my picture of hospitality fit in a new culture? In our first home overseas when our first guests for dinner came over the man finished eating in about five minutes and left the table. I sat there wondering what I had done wrong. We found out later that he was honoring us as hosts saying we had met his needs, he was content.

Of course, we won't be able to know what all our expectations are, but thinking through them as much as we are able would be extremely helpful for us and our cultural adaptation. Once we arrive and we are feeling disappointed or upset, it would be wise to take a minute and ask ourselves, "Why am I angry and what was I expecting?" I think we will find that it is because an unknown expectation wasn't met. In one sense, we need to earn the right to be heard in our host cultures. But we also need to go in as learners, not only of their culture and language, but also in areas such as how to build relationships. We must seek to understand them and listen to them.

A related expectation is that 50 percent of survey respondents went into new cultures expecting to enjoy national friendships, but reality did not match their expectations. Though we don't usually notice since it happens so gradually and naturally, it takes time to build friendships in our home country. How much more time it will take with friends from other cultures, especially because they have their friends and family nearby and usually do not feel a need to befriend us. Building relationships will require a purposeful investment on our part and is so much more than just talking and sharing our message.

When my husband and I were visiting a North African country, a pleasant man greeted us and was very friendly. He invited us for tea and again we were impressed with his friendliness! He took us to a carpet shop and proceeded to show us carpet after carpet in hopes that we would buy one. We were surprised. He wasn't being friendly to us; he wanted our business! (I hope that in my efforts to share the gospel with people that I never look at them as merely prospective "customers" for my message, but rather friends to share my life with no matter their response to the gospel message.) One frustration that missionary women have shared is that they expected to make friends, but didn't expect to have to try to figure out if it was friendship that was wanted in return, or money, help with a green card or another favor. One woman expressed her frustration not only with her thwarted expectation of learning the language and ministering effectively, but also with wondering about her friends' motives in building their relationship:

> I thought it would be easier to learn the language deeply enough to share about eternal issues. I didn't expect to experience so many feelings of personal failure in this, or the fear that seemed to be the root. I thought nationals would desire my friendship for who I was, not what I could give to them monetarily.

On the other hand, we cannot become cynical or suspicious of everyone's motives. Read what Robynn experienced when it came to giving and receiving:

> There is a Hindu teacher who lives on our property. He serves as our landlord's family teacher. They call him Pandit Ji. He advises them spiritually. They provide for him physically. This relationship has been going on for over 30 years. About nine months before we left India, Pandit Ji's wife broke her leg back in the village. It was a pretty severe break and required a steel rod to support the fracture and to expedite the healing. However, medical conditions are poor in the village and her leg became infected. They brought her into our city to see

a specialist. She was admitted to a local hospital and quite quickly it was decided that they needed to redo the surgery to remove the rod.

Such procedures involve money. Pandit Ji quickly taxed his limited resources. The landlord's family gave, but not as much as Pandit Ji thought they should. He soon arrived at our door asking for money. Lowell and I both felt we should certainly give. This poor, elderly, illiterate woman from the village was in absolute agony. She was suffering. Her leg had turned septic and she was in a great deal of pain. Pandit Ji asked for more money and we gave him more. His wife needed more days in the hospital, more medicine, more higher-powered antibiotics, more IV solution, more sterile bandages. These things required more money. She was eventually discharged, but still there were needs. A doctor had to come each day to check her leg, change dressings and administer another, stronger antibiotic.

During this time Lowell visited her; I visited her. We prayed over her. We had other people join us in praying for her. We took guests over there to pray for her. Lowell brought in another doctor to get another opinion. He suggested a slightly different approach, but Pandit Ji wasn't convinced. Our suggestions were not followed. Still we prayed on. And we gave more. And others gave. Other visitors passing through heard the story, met the woman and they, too, were moved with compassion and they gave. It was so hard to know what to do. Eventually we gave almost all we had. We really gave until it hurt.

Cash flow was the problem. The move from India to the U.S. meant a lot of additional expenses. Financially it was a bit of a nightmare. And we really were emptied out. We had no more to give.

And then Pandit Ji came one more time. He entered the courtyard door and called to us. I was in the kitchen, I heard him and my heart sank. I called Lowell and the three of us sat down under the mango tree. Pandit Ji, once again explained that the pharmacy had been giving him medicines on credit but now the shopkeeper really needed to be paid. They were threatening to not release any more painkillers or antibiotics or bandages until the bill was settled. It seems to me, the bill was for 26,000 rupees. That was a lot. Lowell and I looked at each other. We explained to Pandit Ji how our money was all used up. Pandit Ji couldn't hear or couldn't believe that we as North Americans had come to the end of our resources. Lowell opened up his Bible and told the story of Peter and John at the temple gate and their response to the needy lame man, "silver and gold have I none." Suddenly an internal Holy Voice reminded me that there was still more I could give. It wasn't true that we didn't have silver or gold. I did. I had my gold bangles. The voice of God very clearly led me in that moment to strip off my bangles and to hand them over to Pandit Ji.

Those bangles had been given to me two years earlier for my birthday. It was an outrageous gift. They were from a teammate who simply wanted to give me something elaborate. She really didn't have reason. She felt it was the gift to be given. And I of course was thrilled to receive them. I grew up in Asia. Asians love gold. They were 22-karat gold with red and green enamel worked into their pattern. I loved those bangles.

But God was asking me to give them away. Just when you think you've poured out all you possibly can … The gift of the bangles meant something to Pandit Ji. He assumed they were my wedding gold. He understood the sacrifice and the significance involved. And still, even after giving him the gold bangles, Pandit Ji came again asking for money. His situation was relentless. He was desperate. It was so hard.

Indians were ruled by the Moguls, the Maharajas and then the British. Sometimes they may tend to have a poverty complex as a result. They often expect to be given things by the bigger power. The *burra loag* give to the *chota loag*. The big people, the people in power or authority or wealth give to the smaller people, or the people with needs, or the people lower than the bigger people. It's a funny system to me, but it seems to be deeply engrained in their psyche.

Many, many times we've been asked for money. Our white complexions don't help the situation. Assumptions are made and then requests are made. It was certainly not within my expectations or my experience to ever receive money from an Indian!

Imagine then with me my absolute shock one evening when Raju asked me if he could speak to me privately. We were hosting a team of believers from a different city. I had met the Pastor at a wedding in South Asia. He was intrigued by our ministry in the North and asked about the possibility of bringing a short-term team from his church to do street evangelism and prayer in our city for a week. We were thrilled by this idea. A group eight came. Many of them had never been outside their hometown; many more had never been out of the south. They were horrified by the intense Hinduism. They were shocked by the number of idols and temples. It was an eye-opening experience for them. Bobby, one of the young guys on the team who worked in a big city as an IT programmer called his mother to relieve some of her fears. She was so worried about where they would stay and what they would eat. It was as if they had come to a foreign country.

They stayed in the Ashram. We fed them and helped show them around. They did some ministry on the streets of our town but also down by the river. A local pastor also had them come to the other side of the river to do some speaking in the villages around our city.

On their last night with us we were debriefing them in our living room. I was just on my way to go and get the *chai* and the coffee when Raju asked if he could speak to me privately. He respectfully called me Auntie and in my stomach I just knew he was going to ask me for money. This is how it always happened.

I sighed internally and asked him to accompany me to the kitchen to get the drinks. When we reached the kitchen, his voice lowered to a whisper and he pulled out of his pocket a wad of rupees. Would I please take this money and give a thousand rupees to Pastor Akshay, give a thousand rupees to the Ashram and would I please take a thousand rupees for our own ministry? He was quiet and kind. It was a huge amount for him. He was making sacrifices and being obedient to the Holy Spirit. Tears came into my eyes. I felt so terrible for judging him prematurely and cruelly. I thanked him humbled and sobered by the reality of God to lead people into generosity and obedience. Preconceived theories were blown away by the breath of the Spirit at work in His people!

God works through peoples of all cultures to work His purposes for His glory. Each of us must keep looking to Him to work in us and through us wherever we live and however we serve.

Another area where westerners, and maybe others, struggle to adapt is in the area of privacy. Many times we are used to some privacy and expect we will have it in our new culture, only to find that there are no secrets. In one country where we lived people would bring home purchases at night for privacy, but

133

neighbors would still know! When our family went to the zoo we went expecting to have a nice day as a family. We quickly realized as people gathered around to stare at us that we were part of the exhibit! They were curious about us and wanted to see what we would do. There are certain questions that are impolite to ask in some cultures that are expected to be asked in others, certain subjects that are spoken of more freely in some cultures than others. One newlywed friend was constantly asked by her neighbor if she was pregnant yet. This was only slightly embarrassing until she was actively trying to become pregnant. After months and months of trying, having someone keep asking if she was pregnant was a terrible pressure to bear.

Members of a host culture can make assumptions about matters, like pregnancy, which are considered private in a missionary's home culture. Robynn shares a story of how her friends expected her to have a baby:

> We arrived in our city eight months after our wedding day. Almost exactly. We were married on May 7, 1994 and we stepped off the train on to the station platform on January 15, 1995. I had lost a lot of weight before our wedding date, not necessarily intentionally but from residual sicknesses as a result of my visit to South Asia in January 1994. My wedding dress was a size 8. The first year of marriage was coupled with support-raising, lots of travel, meals shared with kind friends and family, last North American treats consumed with perceived deprivation on the horizon. There was a lot of eating. However I did manage to keep things down to a size 10…. ok, maybe a couple of pairs of pants were a size 12. And then there was that size 14 skirt! But mostly, I had not completely lost it in the weight department.

> Very soon after our arrival, the local house fellowships gathered for a conference. At one point during the conference, I sat

cross legged with a group of other women on the floor. I had a sari on and most of the requisite jewelry and bridal markings. I was the new bride and they knew it. There was tittering and teasing, a great deal of curiosity and questions. One older lady asked when we had been married. I told her it was last May. She nodded knowingly and the rest of the group joined her. They smiled and nodded.

I was a little perplexed but then the older lady explained what everyone in the group but me already knew: I would have a baby any time now. It had been 10 months since my marriage and the first baby always came in that first year. Soon, I would have a baby. I laughed and said no glancing down at the stomach I had managed to keep flat ... I wasn't expecting a baby any time soon. They laughed louder, and the nodding started up again. Oh yes, I would have a baby any time now!

There are not only expectations from the host culture, but unsolicited words of "encouragement" and counsel when you are doing something *wrong*. You are not meeting their expectations. Advice that is given so freely may be seen as intrusive in some cultures and caring in others. There is advice on how to dress a baby, what to wear, how often to rest, how to care for family, how soon to go out once you've had a baby and what to do if you are sick. When I am sick in my home country, I expect to be by myself to a certain extent so I can rest and recuperate. In other countries that is unheard of; it would be cruel to leave someone who is ill alone. So when a person is sick, there is always someone nearby. Many of these expectations are so ingrained from birth that when they are unmet or infringed upon, we are taken by surprise. It is easy to get angry and to assume the motives behind unwanted actions to be bad, since our culture and practices are so different from theirs.

Another problem facing many women missionaries is the lack of a safe place to exercise or to do something she enjoys. One aspect of this is simply the time to do it; however another aspect is that in many cultures women do not jog in public or exercise in a mixed-gender gym. Being prepared for this will help, but it can still be a struggle. Expecting to stay physically fit when exercise options are limited in a new culture can produce anxiety. Without exercise, there is no good way to relieve that anxiety. To help solve this problem, some missionary women have started women's gyms, others bring DVDs and work out in their homes and others find culturally appropriate ways to exercise like bicycling for transportation.

National friends have other expectations of us, some of which are due to stereotypes. Some Middle Easterners expect North American women to be immoral, as they are in some movies and television shows. My husband and I found that people were afraid at first to come to a party in our home, assuming I would serve pork, drink liquor or try to seduce their husbands. It was only after they got to know us that they realized the stereotypical view they had of all American women was faulty. They also had many other expectations of Americans: all Americans are rich; all Americans have two children. I remember many taxi rides where the driver would ask us where we were from. When we answered America, their response was that we couldn't be since we had four children!

When asked about the roles of missionary women in their Middle Eastern country, Ruba Abbassi reported in an article for Christar that some national believers were quite skeptical of the missionary women's contributions. They felt that missionary women sometimes did not adequately understand the language or culture, held different values and did not fully understand Arab women. Middle Eastern women would like to feel that missionary women respect them and their culture, but at times they had the perception that the foreigners felt superior to them.

Another area of expectations members of our host culture might have for us is regarding our roles. In interactions with national leadership, there can be confusion as to what a woman's role might be. One surveyed woman wrote, "The demands put on me by established 'national' leaders was very stereotypical and not at all who I was. When I worked with new believers and starting reaching out on my own, it was more fruitful and fulfilling." It is good to work where we are gifted. However, I also wonder what the thoughts and feeling were of her national leaders, how they communicated together about the changes she made and if there was an effect on their relationship. It might be necessary to work through some of the role issues through discussion, and using creativity. The leader and the missionary might look together at what needs to be done and collaborate on how to accomplish their goals. Looking at what they would like to see happen, seeking to understand where the other is coming from and coming up with new ideas while seeking to be sensitive to and understanding of each other's cultures are important.

Whether we are looking at our expectations for our new culture or theirs of us as missionaries, there are plenty on both sides to be addressed. The important thing is that these expectations are dealt with and addressed. One thing that missionaries can do is go ready to learn from nationals. With all of our training and preparation to go overseas, we must sometimes appear as over confident and superior to those we are trying to reach. However, I remember Robynn's husband Lowell saying that at a gathering of national believers in South Asia he noticed one older gentleman that others seemed to respect a great deal. He went up to him to talk and asked him to pray for him and ask God to bless his ministry. Westerners do not have all of the answers and we need to humbly learn from national brothers and sisters. Rather than ignoring established churches, can more ways be found to partner with them rather than separate from them? We learned a great deal sitting under the teaching of a national pastor who took the time to invest in us and share with us what he had learned in his many years of ministry. National leaders can be patient and also seek to work with us, getting to know our strengths and gifts. It would be wise to not assume what we can do and what we are like, but to take the time needed to understand where we are coming from and what we would like to see happen for God's glory.

We also must remember that unmet expectations can lead to anger and bitterness. Negative emotions that continue unchecked have a definite role in a missionary succumbing to burnout.

Survival Tip #7
Heaven is our home

It was by faith that Abraham obeyed when God called him to leave home and go to another land that God would give him as his inheritance. He went without knowing where he was going. And even when he reached the land God promised him, he lived there by faith—for he was like a foreigner, living in tents… Abraham was confidently looking forward to a city with eternal foundations, a city designed and build by God.

> … All these people died still believing what God had promised them. They did not receive what was promised, but they saw it all from a distance and welcomed it. They agreed that they were foreigners and nomads here on earth. Obviously people who say such things are looking forward to a country they can call their own. If they had longed for the country they came from, they could have gone back. But they were looking for a better place, a heavenly homeland. That is why God is not ashamed to be called their God, for he has prepared a city for them. (Hebrews 11:8-10, 13-16, NLT)

Over the years I (Robynn) have warned many a person applying for career missions that once they leave for the field their lives are ruined forever. Never again will they feel fully at home any where. They'll arrive in their new country to serve and will always feel (or be made to feel), even after years of living there, like the foreigner that they are. Returning to their passport country with excitement at the prospect of finally going "home," they'll perpetually feel just a little out of it—or they won't be sure they actually want to feel at home anymore in a country of such materialism, busyness and seeming apathy.

Marrying Lowell the issue of where we were really from and where our home really was could have confused us. I had grown up in Pakistan. I had a Canadian passport. Lowell was an American citizen and was serving in South Asia. Where would our home be? Right from the beginning we cultivated the mantra and lived in its reality that Heaven is our true Home. We've persuaded our children. We've drilled it in to them. Where is home? Heaven!

A friend gave us a wall hanging that reads, "Home is where your story begins." On one level that is true I suppose. But consider if you've grown up in an abusive home, in a broken home, in and out of the foster care system. Home isn't there. Home is where we're going. It's that place that welcomes us in and accepts us. There'll be no more separation, no more grief. In the face of burnout perhaps the most comforting thought about Heaven is the rest that we are promised. Rest. Eternal and complete.

Jesus is at home. His hospitality will embrace us and remove all shame and guilt. We'll leave all of our strivings and all of our anxieties. What has been so blurry and confused will be suddenly clear and obvious.

Take some time to meditate on heaven. Look up the following passages and reflect on what they say about heaven, about our true citizenship, about our inheritance, about the waiting. If you begin to feel homesick that's OK. Communicate that longing to Jesus. He's excited to have us home, too. He understands that feeling because He knows that Heaven is our Home!

THE ROADMAP TO SURVIVAL

(I highly recommend the New Living Translation! These verses come alive in that particular version.)

- Hebrews 11: 8-16

- 2 Peter 1:11 Imagine the "grand entrance!"

- 1 Peter 1:3-7 Linger on, "So be truly glad. There is wonderful joy ahead…"

- Colossians 3:1-4

- Philippians 1:27

- 2 Corinthians 4:16-18

- 2 Corinthians 5:1-5 "..when this earthly tent we live in is taken down…" !

- Romans 8:15-17

- Revelations 5:6-14

- Revelations 21:1-7

EIGHT

THE EXPLORATION CONTINUES, EXPECTATIONS AND GOD

"Disappointment with God does not come only in dramatic circumstances. For me, it also edges unexpectedly into the mundaneness of everyday life." – Philip Yancey

Soon after arriving overseas I discovered that my expectations of God were tightly wound up with the expectations I had for myself. I had a plan and I wanted God to fit into it. I did not recognize this at first, but as my expectations were not being met, I had to look at their root.

Why wasn't God using me to lead hundreds of women to Jesus Christ? I didn't do that in America, but I expected this to change. Now it was my career, my calling! Why wasn't God making my family perfect in every way? I didn't realize that these were the expectations I had of myself and ultimately of God until they weren't fulfilled. God was not fitting into my plans. How much of these expectations was sinful ambition and how much they grew out of a desire to honor God is hard to say, but my expectations were high. I really wanted God to be seen in my life; I desired to be spiritually dynamic. I wanted God to work in me and through me so I would have miraculous stories to tell; I wanted Him to make me fluent in the language so I could minister effectively across cultures. My expectations of myself and of God were entangled.

I was not alone. According to the survey, many other missionary women have these same high, often unrealistic, expectations and they are not met. These are expectations of themselves, but ultimately I think they are also tied to expectations of God to help them reach miraculous goals. They end up being not only disappointed in themselves, but also in God. On the other hand, women also need to work through what they expect of themselves and how that might be intertwined with what they think God expects of them and what God does indeed expect of them. Notice these comments from two women who responded to the survey, how they dealt with unfulfilled expectations and what they learned about themselves and God:

> It was hard. Language did not come easily; the work is slow; people can sometimes be harsh. At times God seemed far away. Doubts have crept in about calling. Supporters in the USA ... couldn't understand why tens of thousands were not coming to know Christ. In the end, by reexamining my calling, I've seen that God just expects us to be faithful and hold on to the end. Don't look at others for our affirmation.

> When I started I had no kids. Now I have three. I find that I have less time to learn language, less time to be involved in ministry outside the home and I have less visitors/friends as a result. That's frustrating sometimes, and I have to let go of that and realize that this is for a season. As well, I have to continually remind myself not to compete or compare (with teammates, with my husband) ... I want to expect myself to be able to do all of these things well, but if I don't get to them or can't get to them, I try to let it go and realize that God has reasonable expectations of me so I shouldn't make unreasonable expectations of myself.

Through their experience in cross-cultural ministry, these women were reevaluating what were real expectations of themselves, others and God, and what were only perceived ones. As we try to figure this out it is imperative that we look to God for guidance. Of course, while we pursue a thriving relationship with God, we discover that no matter how spiritual we are, how faithful we are, we are always aware of our faults and failings. The question we must ask ourselves is, can we ever achieve the level of spirituality we would desire? When I was younger I remember thinking how great it would be to be older and more spiritually mature. However, as I matured, I grew ever more aware of my sinful heart. So if we persist in having high expectations of ourselves and God regarding what we should be like, even as we grow and mature, we may find ourselves unable to achieve the ideal we have set up in our own minds.

Similarly, those who work for years without seeing any tangible results may become painfully aware that they have unmet expectations of themselves and God. Do they need to make changes? Pray more? Work harder? Develop a different strategy? Leave that area and go somewhere more receptive? Or do they just need to persevere and keep working? Keep proclaiming? Keep at it? Never give up? What is it that God is expecting from us? Are we letting Him down? I found the lack of tangible results to be a most irksome problem as I worked among least-reached peoples. Was I making any difference? If I was, how was I? If I wasn't, why wasn't I? I expected God to do something. Big. Where was He in the midst of all the uncertainty?

It has been oddly comforting, as I've talked with other missionaries, to know that I am not alone in feeling disappointed with God. Sometimes I wish God would simply zap me and make me spiritual and fruitful, confident in ministry, a trailblazer for Him. I also admit that I could go through all 34 expectations on the survey and put a four by each one; I always thought I should be good at everything! Wouldn't that be what God would want?

How do I separate my expectations of God, what He should do or be like, from my expectations of myself and what I want to accomplish for Him. And so we come back to the question, what does He expect of me?

In the end what nearly pushed me (It's my turn now. This is Robynn.) over the edge were both my expectations of God and my understanding of His expectations of me. These were the landmines of my missionary career. God disappointed me so profoundly and on so many occasions, and I lived under the weight of knowing that I was disappointing Him as well. It was a maddening circle of thought that spiraled downward and took me down as well.

We all know it's true. God has expectations of the believer. He expects us to be loving and kind, to be servants of one another, to bear one another's burdens. Doesn't Scripture tell us that we are also to take up our crosses, to die to ourselves, to be living sacrifices? Are we not supposed to always give ourselves to the work of the Lord? Are we not supposed to seek first the Kingdom of God? These are the things I knew and I tried so hard to obey them. I really thought I was taking up my cross. I thought I was sacrificing in all the right ways. I thought I was. But it was such a weight to live under. It wore me down. It pushed me down. The cross is heavy and it hurts to carry it for long distances. I fell often and the cross fell on top of me and pinned me down. I didn't experience the light burden and yoke of it all that Jesus promised and that disappointed me.

Rarely did God swoop in and rescue me. Rarely did He live up to my expectations of Him. I believed Him for so many things. I took Him at his word for protection, for joy, for safety. I prayed and prayed, pleaded and pleaded and yet often He didn't answer. He didn't come through.

Ronny and Annie Mishra had been married for 12 years but they hadn't been able to have any children. They had tried all kinds of treatments and tricks, both spiritual and medical, to no avail. Their marriage struggled through their infertility. Indian culture is merciless to the barren woman. Annie knew she was a disappointment to Ronny and to her mother-in-law. She felt it. They let her know it. It was agonizing.

During this time some believing friends of ours, the Nicklesons, moved into their neighborhood. Donnie and Beth befriended Ronny and Annie. The four of them naturally got along and enjoyed one another. Donnie and Beth had also struggled through infertility and were in the process of adopting from an orphanage in a nearby town. The Mishras walked with them through that experience. When little Achal joined the Nickleson family, all four of them celebrated her arrival. Beth also introduced them to another couple who came to faith and then miraculously had a child. This resonated with Ronny and Annie. What kind of amazing God was this who gave children to the childless? We all prayed fervently and slowly the seeds of faith began to grow in their hearts. God was doing it! He was answering prayer.

In great faith we all began to pray that the Mishras would have a baby. We prayed. Oh, how we prayed. We believed it would happen. I could imagine a little baby in Annie's arms. I knew God was going to do this for them. It was thrilling to watch it unfold.

And then Annie called me. Her period was late! She was ecstatic. So was I! Praise rolled off her tongue. She couldn't believe how good God was. How miraculously He was answering her prayers. She and Ronny were full of faith and joy and optimism!

Three days later she called again. Annie was quiet, subdued and full of sorrow. Her period had started. She was not pregnant. She was not expecting that small baby that she had already imagined herself grooming and loving and cuddling. That baby had died. I grieved with her on the phone. I assured her of God's love and persistent care for her. I told her it still could happen. God would give them a child. I recommended she call Beth who was in the U.S. at that time.

As soon as I was off the phone, I pitched a huge spiritual temper tantrum! How could God do this? Did He not see how great an impact this was having on Annie, on their marriage, on Ronny's heart, on the mother-in-law? Did He not realize what a great thing this would be for the whole community? His glory would spread through that neighborhood like wildfire. Wasn't that what He was after? What was He thinking?

There was also the time our landlord's servant girl became really ill. We had been praying that God would do whatever it would take for our landlord's family to come to faith. Every time we mentioned Jesus to them there was a perceptible glazing over of their eyes. They were blinded and we knew that unless the Spirit of God did a work nothing we could do would amount to any change in their souls. So we waited to see what God might do.

Savitri, their servant girl, came down with hepatitis, and then typhoid. Her condition worsened and she was quite quickly hospitalized. Here was the opportunity for God to work in the way that we had been hoping.

At the same time we had a short-term team from Vancouver visiting us. They were keen young college kids with fervent faith and a desire to be used by God. Just before their departure from Canada, a woman had approached them with a prophetic word. She felt in her spirit that God was going to use them to pray prayers for healing and that He would do it! It was a simple message and it gave the team a great deal of anticipation thinking of who God might heal. The first night they were with us, we were all sitting on the roof of our house watching the Ganges River. Lowell told the team about Savitri and asked them to pray for her healing. He further charged them to pray for our landlord's family. The team was primed to pray such prayers. They believed firmly that God would heal.

The next day Lowell went to the hospital. He had been going regularly to see Savitri, to give blood and to pray, but on this particular day he boldly asked if he might lay hands on her and ask God for her healing. The family priest, Pandit Ji, was there on one side of the bed. Lowell stood on the other side. In true Old Testament Elijah-versus-prophets-of-Baal fashion, Lowell reached out and prayed for Savitri's full healing. In true New Testament, Jesus-among-us style Savitri sat up and asked for something to eat! It was unbelievable! It gave us all goose bumps. God was healing her!

Later that afternoon, our landlord Vinay, came by to tell me the whole story and to have some tea. As we were chatting He said something like this: "It's amazing. Jesus is healing Savitri! Lowell Ji prayed and she sat up and asked for food! Jesus is healing her. Lowell prayed and he gave blood. And I had special pujas done for her at the monkey temple and here at the kali temple. I've paid all this money just for a servant girl and I've hired all these good doctors to care for her. And I sent Pandit Ji to watch over her at the hospital ..." Vinay went on and on about how God was healing her but also more about all the good works he himself had done to bring this healing about. He started to take credit for it. As I listened to him, a dread slowly filled my stomach. I quickly exhorted Vinay, "No, Vinay, It is Jesus who is healing her. Jesus alone. Do not think it is anything you are doing. Jesus is very jealous of His glory. Be sure to give Him all the credit for this." "Yes, Yes," he assured me, but it wasn't sincere; and once again his eyes glazed over.

The next day Savitri died. I was so angry at God. God had promised to heal her. And it looked like He was ... but then ... death? What was He doing? We had imagined how this healing would ricochet in our landlords' family, in our neighborhood, in our community, amongst these young college kids, in our own hearts, in the hearts of our three children. And just when it seemed God was doing it, He clearly changed His mind. I was devastated. We all were. What went wrong? We prayed prayers in faith, exuberant faith even. We really believed He would do it. He let us down.

In December 2004, Lowell wrote a prayer letter:

On September 1, Robynn and I awoke with an overwhelming sense of the need to minister to Shivraj and his family, this 6-year-old boy of our landlord who was dying of aplastic anemia, the inability of his bone marrow to produce new platelets and blood cells. Now, we had been ministering—praying for his healing, recruiting prayers, giving blood, giving money, and giving comfort and encouragement. But that Wednesday, our ministry sense was that we needed to prepare this boy and his family for the possibility that the Great God of Heaven might not heal him, that in fact he might die. So that afternoon, Robynn and I sat down and talked with Shivraj's parents and his aunt and uncle. We did not spare a single item of the good news nor of the harsh realities. In fact, we frankly told the family that while it is a very religious thing that they had done in giving blood sacrifices to Kali, their family goddess, these past 800 years, that all those sacrifices have been unnecessary. Jesus, the perfect sacrifice, once for all, shed His blood for our salvation. We told them that, in our estimation, Kali, the most bloodthirsty of the Hindu pantheon, was requiring the blood of their son Shivraj this year. After all, they had given Shivraj to her. We explained that while Kali takes blood, Jesus gives blood—His own. We explained that Jesus might heal Shivraj in answer to our prayers, but he is God, and may choose not to. Even so, we are not without hope—Jesus' heaven is a place of joy, life and healing. Either way, the need is the same—they must take their son from Kali and give him to Jesus. We left a Hindi Bible and a children's Bible.

That evening, our Sangati (fellowship) came over and prayed for Shivraj. Even his parents joined in, calling upon the name of Jesus.

The next day, Robynn and I were exhausted. We could barely even get out of bed. We dragged listlessly through the entire day. That night, I climbed up on the roof before bedtime in order to say a few quick prayers. Immediately, a spirit of joy and exhilaration came upon me. I started praising the Lord from some internal source of new energy. I had two senses—of which I'll share one here. I sensed that the Lord was telling me that Shivraj had been successfully transferred from the hands of Kali to the hands of Jesus. Now, Jesus might heal him. But He might not. Jesus might save his soul. But He might not. AND YET—Jesus is gracious and compassionate, slow to anger and abundant in lovingkindness. He is altogether trustworthy. God's will is not always our will, but His will is always good. All our prayers had been answered. Shivraj was exactly where he was supposed to be.

In the week that followed, Shivraj's condition improved. In the second week, it deteriorated rapidly. Interestingly, during these two weeks, I tried to pray for Shivraj, but found a gentle block in my soul. I felt the Lord saying, "Why pray further? I've already answered and given you what you want." During those two weeks, Shivraj's family, including his staunchly Hindu grandmother, read to Shivraj the stories of Jesus in the children's Bible.

On Wednesday, September 15, I visited Shivraj in the hospital where he had been taken for another blood transfusion. He was greatly uncomfortable. That afternoon, Robynn woke me up from a nap with the news, "Shivraj has passed away." We went next door. Within a couple hours, while Robynn stayed with the violently grieving women, I joined the men, barefoot, as we took Shivraj's small body down to the Ganges River, where we wrapped it in an ornate cloth, tied a stone to it and dumped it in the river.

That very day, in response to the heart-wrenching question of Shivraj's mother, Robynn had occasion to ask her, "Did you ever give Shivraj to Jesus?" She replied, "Yes, I did. I really did."

She did and yet God let us down. Again. At least that's how it felt to me.

George Uncle, the most promising leader to take over the church, died of leukemia. Munnu and Gita did not come to faith. Kristen had another miscarriage. Gautum and Archna heard the gospel from many of us and yet they didn't ever believe it. Our friend Donnie kept getting sick. Jenna caused troubles on her team and wouldn't admit it. Don kept trying to control how things would go. Auntie professed faith and then threw a huge puja party for another god in hopes of things working out for her mentally troubled son. People came to faith and fell back in to unbelief. My dad, in a neighboring country, was a victim of a terrorist attack and lost his hearing.

When God has not answered the prayers I've prayed in the ways I would have wanted him to, many well-meaning people have told me over the years that I should take comfort in the fact that He alone is in charge. That He alone can change people's hearts. That only He has the power to transform. That only God is sovereign. I suppose that on one level that is comforting. But on another level it's maddening. He asks us to go in to the harvest to gather it up and to work there. We do our part, but many times it seems He doesn't do His.

I thought I knew God better. I thought that He would be the one thing that would not disappoint. But He did, repeatedly. I could have blamed many of the things that brought pain on circumstances or on other people, and yet I knew that at the end of the day, God is Sovereign. He certainly had control over what happened. He was governing my discipleship, my journey. When each pain was pushed to its source, there stood God.

Back in Bible College I had learned that holiness means "set apart" or "other." God is set apart from us. He is different. But after years in South Asia I came to understand that holiness also means strange. God is weird. When the prophet Isaiah says that God's ways are different than our ways and God's thoughts are higher than our thoughts, what he was trying to tell us is that God is weird. His ways are so completely different from ours that they appear disastrous and often don't make any sense. But that is holiness. That's the type of ground that burning bushes grow out of. We take our shoes off and we shake our heads.

I know now that my expectations of God were faulty. I didn't expect a rose garden, but neither did I expect that the disappointments and the pains would be so relentless, so incessant, so continuous. I didn't look for a life that would eventually be written up in hard-backed biography, but I did sort of expect a little bit of success, a little bit of visible fruit. I looked for God to rescue me and release me from the hurt of it all. And that's not how God works. I know that now. God *is* strange and weird. His ways *are* perplexing and hard pressing. He's in this for His glory. Somehow mysteriously we get to be a part of that. We get to watch. And His glory *will* shine! Stand back. See the bigger picture. There is a story of redemption and grace at work all around us. In the messiness of the details He is there … deeply devoted to us, deeply at work in us—redeeming and gracing us, too. But all of that happens best in the space of suffering. I didn't expect that. I wasn't looking for that.

I know now that I was also confused about His expectations of me. He wasn't ignoring me. My needs were not less important to Him. He did expect that I would lay down my life, it is what he asked me to do, but he was laying down next to me, intimately inviting me in to deeper and deeper relationship with Him. He was swooping me up and affectionately calling me His own. I am His toddler child. He is my Father. He sees all the children in the room and he doesn't say, "Come on, Robynn, let's help all these other kids out. They are really hurting." That's what I thought He was saying. No. He tenderly calls me over to Him and offers me His lap and then His shoulder and He comforts me.

*   *   *   *   *   *   *   *

How do we respond to these kinds of accounts and experiences? Do we go into cross-cultural ministry not expecting anything of ourselves or God? Do we take any and all expectations and water them down until we can merely survive overseas and think we are successful? Do we keep expecting God to work and when He doesn't, at least according to our desires, do we become so disappointed and emotionally exhausted that we are more apt to burn out? Do we work harder ourselves to try to fulfill our expectations of God and eventually burn out because we cannot do what God can do?

The question that needs to be answered—the bottom line— seems to be this one question: How can we embrace a sometimes harsh and below-our-expectations reality and still expect that our awesome, powerful, almighty God will work in and through us?

Survival Tip #8
Leave room for God

Early one morning, Lowell was on our roof having his quiet time; I (Robynn) was in the courtyard. Suddenly he starts reading from Dallas Willard:

> What we most learn in his yoke [the easy yoke of Christ, (Mt. 11:28-30)], beyond acting with him, is to abandon outcomes to God, accepting that we do not have in ourselves—-in our own "heart, soul, mind, and strength"—the wherewithal to make this come out right, whatever "this" is.
>
> We simply have to rest in his life as he gives it to us. Knowledge, from Christ, that he is good and great enables us to cast outcomes on him. We find this knowledge in the yoke of Christ. Resting in God, we can be free from all anxiety, which means deep soul rest. Whatever our circumstances, taught by Christ we are enabled to "rest [be still] in the Lord and wait patiently [or longingly] for Him" (Psalm 37:7).[1]

We were to "abandon outcomes" to God. Later the same week a teammate who is also a dear friend, Leslie, came over for a cup of coffee. She talked about the need to leave room for God.

Maybe it was not part of God's plan that Ronnie and Annie have a baby. Maybe the only way they would truly pursue Him was if there was that visibly empty space in their family.

---

1   Excerpt from Abandoning Outcomes, Willard, Dallas. (2002). Renovation of the heart. New Press, Colorado Springs CO. (p. 209-210)

All of my striving to fix their problem (fund raisers for further treatment, dropping everything to rush over and comfort and pray, frantically trying to make calls to others to intervene with counsel, interceding to God, demanding of God, pleading with God and then begging Him) was counter productive. Maybe it wasn't what God had in mind all along.

Maybe the Glory of God was increased when Savitri died. As much as that didn't make sense to me maybe it was somehow true in the Heavenlies. Perhaps God allowed Shivraj to die so young for the sake of the work He intended to do in the heart of his mother, his aunts and uncles, his grandmother. Possibly George Uncle was taken from us prematurely was because of what God wanted to do in the heart of his widow, in the community, and to our own faith and assumptions.

No amount of my fretting and anxiety thwarted what God was doing. "Abandoning (the) outcomes," or leaving room for God to work, forces me to stop. There is no sense stirring myself up in a frenzy to fix the problem. God has something else in mind. There is nothing I can do to change His plan.

Yes, I can pray. But when my prayers become cajoling, manipulative, magic-invoking, plea bargaining, or demanding, I've crossed the line. Those are not Spirit led prayers. Those are prayers where Robynn thinks she knows best. I lose dignity in praying those types of prayers and much worse those aren't the prayers Jesus himself is praying sitting at the Father's right hand. I would do well to sit and listen in on those prayers. And then join in with them. The Father longs that Ronnie and Annie passionately seek after Him. He keenly desires to spread his glory across the city. He wants the hearts of Shivraj and his mother and extended family more than I do. God is committed to the fledging church along the banks of the Ganges. He knows what's best. I can give it over to Him, keeping in step with Him, as He leads me to minister. Pausing, resting, listening I ask Him what I should do for the

Ronnies and the Annies, the George Uncles and the Shivrajs of the world. I humbly admit I don't know what's best. There is rest in that. We let God off the hook of our own expectations. He doesn't have to act in a certain way, according to our plan. He is God. And we are not. Take a deep breath. Take another. Listen to God. Leave room for Him. He has a plan and it's glorious and perfect.

NINE

THE EXPLORATION CONTINUES, WHEN GOD DOESN'T MEET HER EXPECTATIONS

Our God is wild and untamable. He is expansive and unpredictable. When we say he is holy, we mean he is strange and we do well to take our shoes off. –Robynn Bliss

God is awesome. He does amazing things that astound us. He works miracles at times when we least expect it. He answers prayer. Scripture confirms that He does "exceedingly beyond what we ask or think." He turns things upside down. He transfers us from the kingdom of darkness to the kingdom of light. He provides for us and protects us mightily. He meets our needs. He heals. God takes our breath away with His mercy, grace, power and love. He is God. He does what is best and what He pleases to bring Him the most glory. We trust Him and strive to be unwavering in our faith. Sometimes, though, we don't understand Him. This chapter seeks to address what happens when He doesn't do what we know He can—what happens when He doesn't meet our expectations.

Let me repeat the question from the previous chapter. How can we embrace a sometimes harsh and below-our-expectations reality and still expect that our awesome, powerful, almighty God will work in and through us? To respond, Robynn shares with us some of what she has learned about expectations, trust and God's wild ways:

When I, Robynn, was 9 and Amy Jo was 8, I asked her if she would be my best friend. I accepted the rejection with fortitude. A year later she asked me if I remembered the question I had asked her a year previous. Of course I did. "The answer," she said, "is now yes!"

When I was 29 and Amy Jo was 28, I stood by her hospital bed and watched her enraptured face as she saw her baby daughter for the first time. It was 11 p.m., six hours after her surgery. The hospital was asleep and quiet. Amy had awakened and asked to see her baby. A nurse and I wheeled baby Kiran Hope's cot down three floors to the Neuro ICU. When Amy focused on my face, she smiled in recognition. When she saw the baby, she beamed. "Oh, Kiran, you're so pretty." She listened with pride as I told her about her new daughter, how healthy she was, how she had scored a 10 on the Apgar test. "Kiran, I'm so sorry that I can't be with you these first few days," she apologized, "but I'll have the rest of my life to make it up to you."

Those were some of the last words Amy Jo ever spoke. She slipped into a coma at 4:00 the next morning and died four days later.

The symptoms were sudden and simple: an intense migraine that started on November 11th. After pregnancy-related causes were ruled out, she was referred to a neurologist. The first MRI was done on November 27 and was inconclusive. Further tests, done on the 28th and the 29th revealed she had a large malignant brain tumor. On November 30 at 1:30 p.m. doctors began two operations, first a C-section, followed by brain surgery. Kiran Hope was born at 1:45 p.m. Amy Jo came out of the OR at 5:10 p.m. I had the blessing and privilege of introducing her to the little girl she had longed for later that night.

Amy Jo was a loyal, kindred-spirit friend. She loved Jesus and wanted to be like Him. All she ever wanted was that He be glorified. She was convinced that it was more important to *be* than to *do*. She was frugal and enjoyed simplicity. Little things were big treats for her. She loved beauty and color and texture and saw it all around her: in vegetable carts, bright saris and children's faces. She was a well-read, intelligent woman with opinions that would have shocked some! She was extremely uncompetitive and couldn't hold her own at Scrabble for the world! She was generous and wanted those around her to be happy.

I loved her. And the missing ache is still quite sore.

Those were hard days. It didn't make sense. God had every opportunity to answer those prayers, to heal Amy Jo, to restore her to life, to give Kiran the mother she deserved. But He didn't come through. For months afterwards my faith was shaken. I couldn't understand it all. We had prayed. E-mails went pouring out soliciting prayer from around the world. Mega churches in South Korea prayed in unison; smaller groups of more reserved people prayed together in the U.K. They prayed in Pakistan, North America and Germany. And we prayed in South Asia, fervently. But still God did not heal. And Amy Jo died.

Months later my husband, Lowell, preached a sermon that I hated. He entitled it "Who Forgot to Pray for James?" The text was Acts chapter 12:1-5. "About that time King Herod Agrippa began to persecute some believers in the church. He had James killed with a sword. When Herod saw how much this pleased the Jewish people, he also arrested Peter. Then he imprisoned him …. while Peter was in prison, the church prayed very earnestly for him." We know the story: the prayers of the church swayed God and He arranged for Peter's miraculous deliverance! But was not the church also praying for James? Is there any reason to think they weren't? Of course they were. Believers are being persecuted; the church rises up with prayer and power to beseech the Great God of the Universe to put an end to it. It's what the church does! There is every reason to believe that the believers also prayed for James and others who were equally brutally treated, and yet God allowed James to be murdered and Peter to walk free. It doesn't make any sense. Who can know how God figures these things out?

During his sermon Lowell used an illustration that communicated powerfully to my battered faith. He explained correctly why I don't like swimming in the ocean: there are living things lurking beneath the surface; the waves are unpredictable and splash my face; it's cold and deep; there are undertows and pulls that frighten; it's salty and sandy and alive. I do not like swimming in the ocean. I much prefer a swimming pool, a heated pool at that. The temperature is controlled. You can enter at your pleasure, either the deep end or the shallow end. You can go in as far as you like and then climb back out. Inflate a floating device and float on the top if you choose! The bottom is level and smooth. There are no surprises. Nothing lives in a swimming pool.

And that's the kind of God I would prefer as well: one that is controlled and moderate; a God I can measure and understand. I can enter His depths but only as far as I am comfortable. However that's not the kind of God we have. Our God is an ocean of a God. He is alive and dangerous. There are forces at work below His surface. He alone controls the depths, the sprays, the splashes of His personhood. He woos us to the bottom where the water may appear murky and mysterious. Our God is wild and untamable. He is expansive and unpredictable. When we say he is holy, we mean he is strange and we do well to take our shoes off. The ground is holy and the water is deep.

After his sermon Lowell asked if I would sing a song. The words to the song *Jesus Lover of My soul (It's All About You)* by Paul Oakley still alarm me, "It's all about you Jesus. And all this is for you, for your glory and your fame. It's not about me, as if you should do things my way. You alone are God and I surrender to your ways." A friend, Becky, joined me in singing after that horrible sermon. I would never have gotten through it with out her.

Because it's true. It's all about Jesus, His glory, His fame. Who are we to think that He would do things our way? He alone is God and so we do surrender to Him and to His holy, weird, strange, wild ways!

*   *   *   *   *   *   *
*

Faith. Trust. Hope. No matter what. We recognize our limitations and our dependency on the Lord for all things. We point people to Him. We ask Him to work. We plead with Him to save. We make ourselves available to Him. We carry our crosses and give our lives. We tell others about Him, praying for their souls. Then, we continue to trust, have faith and hope.

Habakkuk said it best in chapter 3, verses 17-19 (NIV) after he questioned God about the violence and treachery he saw and pondered what was going to happen. His faith in God was not dependent on his "success" or his "fruitfulness." His faith was based on who God is.

> "Though the fig tree does not bud
> and there are no grapes on the vines,
> though the olive crop fails
> and the fields produce no food,
> though there are no sheep in the pen
> and no cattle in the stalls,
> yet I will rejoice in the LORD,
> I will be joyful in God my Savior.
> The Sovereign LORD is my strength;
> he makes my feet like the feet of a deer,
> he enables me to go on the heights.

If we do not grapple with this reality of facing unmet expectations while trusting God, I believe the possibility of experiencing burnout dramatically increases. Not only because of how much harder we will work and how we pretend to show faith when our hearts are really filled with doubt, but also because of the unrest in our souls and disparity between expectations and reality.

In the previous chapters we have looked at expectations of missionary women in six different areas. We have discovered through the surveys that there is a gap between expectations and reality for missionary women in these areas. Multiple researchers have noted a connection between unrealistic expectations and burnout. Some think it is stronger than others; but almost all see some correlation. Clarifying and grappling with expectations is a first step in avoiding burnout. The second step is to gain a better understanding of burnout.

Burnout is a word that is probably overused in today's world. Whenever anyone is feeling stress over a period of time she might say, "I'm feeling burned out." What she really means is she is feeling stress or pressure. It is important to comprehend what burnout really is, recognize its symptoms and know how to avoid it.

Burnout, an overall exhaustion, has been defined by Seymour (1995) as "the emotional exhaustion resulting from the stress of interpersonal contact... in which helping professionals lose positive feelings, sympathy, and respect for their clients" (p. 31). Though it is described as emotional exhaustion, it does affect a person holistically. They are more tired physically, more tired mentally and more apathetic spiritually. It is true there are days when everyone feels more tired, more stressed. A woman might rest, take a day off, enjoy a vacation and feel restored. She then is ready to continue to work and finds enjoyment in it once again. Burnout, however, is a more long-term, continual sense of exhaustion which affects a person so severely that she is often unable to carry on normal day to day activities. A person might start to dislike others, feel apathetic and withdraw from ministry. How do we know whether we are working so hard to meet expectations that we are close to burnout or are simply feeling stress? Are we just tired or are we burning out? In order to be able to differentiate, we have to know what the symptoms of burnout are. We will take a look at these in the next chapter.

Survival Tip #9
Trust God through the "if onlys"

"Lord, if you had been here my brother would not have died." This was said not once, but twice by the sisters who had lost their only brother. Clearly they had spoken these words to each other. Mourners who saw Jesus weeping at the gravesite and realized how much Jesus had loved Lazarus said, "Could not this man, who opened the eyes of him who was blind, have kept this man also from dying?" (John 11, NASB)

Mary and Martha had expected Jesus to get the news that their brother was sick and to come. He should have been there to save their brother. They knew He could. But He wasn't even there. He didn't come in time. I'm (Sue) wondering what His disciples thought of Him as they knew that when He heard Lazarus was sick, He intentionally stayed away even longer. They arrived four days after Lazarus had died.

Lazarus was dead. There was no hope. Expectations were dashed. Martha was certain of a future resurrection and knew that Jesus had power. She knew that one day Lazarus would rise from the dead, but she had no expectation that Jesus would bring him back to life that day.

How many times have we thought, "If only God had done this … would do this … if only." We see what we think needs to be done and when it isn't, it is very easy to blame God, to lose hope, to feel despair.

Earlier in John 6 when the disciples heard Jesus talking about eating His flesh, drinking His blood, and coming to the Father many started to leave (v. 66). He asked those near him if they

167

would go as well. Peter asked in verse 68-69, "Lord, to whom shall we go? You have words of eternal life. And we have believed and have come to know that You are the Holy One of God." (NIV) They recognized that no matter how hard things got, how little they understand, no matter how close to despair they might be, they knew that Jesus was the only hope in the midst of it all.

Friends may die, hopes may be dashed. We may be in the midst of a horrific storm. Despair is crouching at our door of our hearts. And then, when we feel that we just might be overcome we remember. Jesus.

Jesus chose to stay away when Lazarus was dying because he had a bigger and better plan to raise him from the dead, to give people yet another opportunity to have faith in Him.

Jesus spoke of His blood and His flesh because He knew that those who followed Him needed to really know Him, not just follow Him for food or to see miracles. He wanted them to choose to have faith in Him even when He was hard to understand.

We choose to look beyond the present with our finite eyes and look to the eternal with our eyes of faith. Yes, we have the encouragement to come boldly to the throne of grace for help. We tell God of our disappointments and ask Him, trust Him, to work, to heal and to save. And like Martha, we proclaim in the midst of our grief, "You are the Christ, the Son of God." And we trust.

TEN

EXPLORING BURNOUT SYMPTOMS AND CAUSES

When our load is greater than our power, we enter into negative margin status, that is, we are overloaded. Endured long-term, this is not a healthy state. Severe negative margin for an extended period of time is another name for burnout. When our power is greater than the load, however, we have margin.
– Richard A. Swenson, MD

We have looked at expectations missionary women have. They have expectations—some met and some unmet—of themselves, their sending church, their sending agency, their host culture and God. When expectations remain high and reality does not match up, a missionary woman may have several responses: she may work harder, give up, alter her expectations or her reality. What she cannot do is nothing. Continuous, unresolved expectations have a direct relationship to burnout. The challenges of cross-cultural life and work added to unmet expectations can lead to mounting stress. Unchecked stress, whether related to expectations or not, leads to burnout.

Missionary women who are aware of burnout and can recognize its symptoms are better able to avoid it. In the beginning stages, burnout symptoms may include more complaining and less enjoyment, disliking people, an urge to withdraw, a judgmental attitude, drug or alcohol abuse, major fights or an inability to take action (Minirth, 1990). Sanford (1982) has his own list of typical symptoms for missionaries to be aware of:

> Difficulty in sleeping; somatic complaints such as weight loss, lack of interest in food, and headaches and gastro-intestinal disturbances; a chronic tiredness of the sort that is not repaired by sleep or ordinary rest and only temporarily alleviated by vacations; low-grade, persistent depression; and a nagging boredom (p. 1).

When missionary women were asked in the survey what symptoms of burnout they had experienced, there were a wide range of answers.

The worst time was a time I felt that I could not breathe, did not want to get out of bed. It was total helplessness. It came at a time when I had been working with a really poor group of people and they basically would not do some of the things I suggested and their kids would be sick and several of them died. My heart hurt so bad that it took awhile before I could face the people again.

… a lack of concern for the lost around me, doubts about God's existence and wondering whether all of this is really worthwhile. During one period … at the height of my burnout I even found myself thinking about death a lot and wishing that my life would just be over. I wasn't going to take my own life, but I had these thoughts where I wished the Mack truck flying around every curve up on the mountain roads would just go ahead and take me out. It sounds awful, but it's true. I am so grateful to God that He spared me and brought me out of that pit I was in.

On the field I have not personally experienced burnout in the eight years I've been there. But I had earlier in my life in the secular business world, which included sleeplessness, weight loss, fatigue, severe depression, poor self-concept, always feeling like I was a failure and that others were disappointed in me. But after recovering from burnout, I learned to recognize warning signs in my life and I work to maintain a healthy balance in all areas of my life and I have accountability partners to help me do that. I carried this way of life with me to the field and it's helped me to have a good experience thus far. That doesn't mean that I don't have stresses or challenges. I do. But I don't allow those things to drag me down as I had in my past.

Burnout affects every area of our lives: physical, emotional, mental and spiritual. It seems most missionary women have a general idea what burnout is and a large percentage have felt close to it. The survey results show that 80 percent of the missionary women who responded have felt close to burnout. This confirms that most missionary women experience extreme stress. Included witihn that 80 percent are the 19 percent who say that they have actually experienced burnout. An additional five percent felt they possibly had experienced it, but weren't sure. These numbers are high and should encourage us to do all that we can to help missionary women deal with stress in a healthy way, as well as to be aware of the symptoms and causes of burnout.

There are numerous inventories available online to help identify burnout. The Maslach Burnout Inventory—General Survey (referred to as MBI), weighs the effects of emotional exhaustion, depersonalization and personal accomplishment (Dyment, 1989). This indicator has become the most widely used research measure of burnout and is the standard tool for measuring burnout (Zalaquett, 1997). One must be qualified to order and certified to evaluate the results. There is also a stress test by Rosalind Forbes in the book "Why Christians Burn Out" by Charles Perry, Jr. (p. 63). The questions help to determine both what job pressures an individual is facing and how much they may be able to tolerate. Such a self-inventory would be a helpful tool for missionary women and their supervisors as part of a yearly evaluation of their health and well-being.

To be truly geared to their missionary women members, mission agencies could develop their own questionnaire as a small part of an annual review. The expectations on the questionnaire listed should reflect what the mission itself expects as well as general expectations missionary women sometimes have of themselves. Including questions about their emotional well-being and how they are responding to their ability to achieve their goals or not would give insight to the mission agency into how the women are doing, as well as help the women themselves evaluate how they are doing. The following format could be used as a basic template that could be adapted to meet an agency's needs:

1. Do you feel expectations of you from the mission are clear? Discuss this with your supervisor.

2. Rank the following areas based on their importance to you (1 would be most important and 7 would be least important):
   My personal overall health _____
   Taking care of my home _____
   Team relationships _____
   Administrative paperwork with headquarters _____
   Financial reporting and accountability _____
   Ministry/mission work _____
   Language learning and cultural adaptation _____

3. Rank the same list of areas as you feel they are of most importance to your mission headquarters (1 would be most important and 7 would be least important):
   My personal overall health _____
   Taking care of my home _____
   Team relationships _____
   Administrative paperwork with headquarters _____
   Financial reporting and accountability _____
   Ministry/mission work _____
   Language learning and cultural adaptation _____
   Discuss similarities and differences with your supervisor.

4. How often do you feel overwhelmed with all that you need to do?
   ____ seldom _____ often _____ constantly

5. What symptoms have you been experiencing that might be related to stress?

6. List five things that you expect of yourself and determine if your expectations are realistic and/or scriptural. Discuss these with your supervisor.

7. List five things that you think your organization expects of you and if you think they are realistic and/or scriptural. Discuss these with your supervisor.

8. What could your mission agency do to help you deal with your expectations and maintain emotional health? What can you do to help your mission agency understand your needs? Discuss this with your supervisor.

Living with a large amount of stress over a prolonged period of time can be serious and lead to burnout. Missionary women who have a good perspective of expectations and reality, and who recognize symptoms of burnout and are aware of its gradual onslaught will be more likely to avoid it. They may avert it not only by evaluating themselves in light of the symptoms of burnout, but also by learning more about its causes.

Before looking more closely at some of the causes of burnout, let's take a look at Robynn's staircase analogy, showing a bit of what she thinks contributes to burnout:

When you first arrive on the field you are in top form! Adrenaline is racing through your veins. Excitement courses through your brain. You've made it! All the years of preparation, all the costs counted, all the sacrifices made, all the bags packed, all the necks hugged, all the farewells bid … you did it! You made it to the field. With sleeves rolled up you are ready to roll. Let your missionary career begin!

You're on the top step of the staircase. Expectations are high.

The first weeks pass. Perhaps you get a case of diarrhea. Perhaps your teammates aren't as considerate as you thought they should be. Perhaps it takes you longer to find a place to live, longer to set it up, longer to stock it with groceries you can cook, longer to cook them than you ever imagined. The novelty has worn off. The adrenaline has slowed. The excitement has waned. You're tired.

You're down a couple of steps….

But no problem! You take a day off. You read a book that inspires; you watch a movie that entertains. You remember why you're in the country, and before you know it you're back up a step—maybe not quite to the top, but almost.

And then language study plateaus. The sounds don't form on your contorted tongue. You have a degree from your home state's university but you can't communicate a simple request in a local restaurant. The people surrounding you are really starting to annoy you. Their habits make no sense. They stare. They smell odd. Their curiosity repels you.

You're down a few more steps …

But no problem. You take a week-long vacation. You drink some comforting beverages. You eat tasty food. You spend long hours in Scripture. You write out things in your journal. You remember why you're there and, before you know it, you're back up a step—maybe not quite where you were, but almost. You feel considerably refreshed …

And then there's conflict on your team. The team leader doesn't understand you. He doesn't take the time to listen to your ideas or learn from your experiences. You feel frustrated and wonder what your role is. And then you're sick with typhoid, or malaria and dengue fever. The fever and its affects wear you down and wear you out. You are weak. You are discouraged.

You're down several more steps …

But no problem! You take a couple of months of home assignment. Surrounded by your loving family and your supportive church, you bask in the treats of your home culture. Worshiping in your mother tongue together with your community of faith is soothing. Your soul begins to heal. Perspective is regained. Your body is strengthened and your spirit recovers. You remember why you were there and before you know it, you return and you're back up several steps. Maybe not quite where you were when you first went out, but almost. You are full of hope.

And then the little boy next door gets sick with a terminal disease. You share Christ and the hope and healing He can bring. You pray over the child and the child rallies for a week or two and then dies. And then a young couple who recently came to faith, disappointed by God not giving them the child they so desperately ached for, suddenly stops coming to church services. They walk away from it all. And then teammates go through a miscarriage. It's the fourth one they've had. Their grief is thick and unbearable.

And then an elder in your fledgling, weak, little church dies of leukemia. All of you had had great hope that he would lead the church after your departure. Even in his illness you had had such faith he would be healed. And now he's gone, along with your dreams and expectations for the church plant. And then you come to know that your house helper has been stealing from you. You feel betrayed and vulnerable and angry . . . and very tired.

And then your children are tormented at school. And then your spouse needs emergency surgery. And then your fridge quits working. And then there is no water for three days. And then your computer gives out. And then someone comes to borrow money for his wife who is sick. And then he comes again to borrow more money. And then your one friend in the city misunderstands you and is upset ... and then ... and then ... and then ...

You are down on the second to last step. You're close to the bottom, more tired than ever before, more weary in well-doing. A day off isn't going to bring much relief. A two-week vacation will bring you up a couple of steps, but the going down is quicker now. The steps are slipperier. It's harder and harder to maintain your ground. Going back up to the top seems nearly impossible. Moments of joy take you up a step. But unanswered prayers, hard work, too many responsibilities, the rigors of life, the constant demands—it all takes its toll. Burnout beckons in the basement, at the bottom of the stairs.

*   *   *   *   *   *   *   *

Many missionaries have felt they were at the bottom of the stairs, but they have not experienced burnout. There are some people with personality traits, background issues and spiritual lives that can help them work through difficult circumstances like Robynn described and still not experience burnout. However, other people have different personality traits, background issues and spiritual lives and may experience less hardship, and yet they burn out. Keeping that in mind, we need to look at factors beyond circumstances contributing to burnout, because if missionaries understand what causes burnout they may be able to avoid it. Continuously unfulfilled expectations and recurring difficult circumstances can make a person more susceptible to burnout. Also, giving more than a person has to offer can lead to burnout. Rediger (1982) puts it well when he writes, "In burnout, one gives away so much of oneself that one cannot fulfill ministry any longer. To persist in efforts to give more than one has to give, no matter how noble, is to set oneself up for burnout" (p. 24). How many missionaries keep giving even when they need to rest? More importantly, how many people admire them and encourage them for doing this? How do boundaries fit in with sacrificing all for the Lord, especially when there are so many needs and not enough personnel to meet them?

People give sacrificially and pray to send missionaries out to serve. Missionaries want to be faithful and work hard since they were commissioned for a task that is of eternal significance. As they work through such questions and priorities, they have to realize when to say no, when to say yes, when to rest and when to keep working. Realizing that setting healthy boundaries is easier said than done, it is wise for missionaries to have some uncommitted time and energy built into their lives. They must know when to keep within their boundaries as well as when to push them. Missionaries can sometimes feel that they give and give of themselves to no avail. After an extended period of such boundless giving, a root of bitterness may begin to grow.

Minirth (1990) comments on the relationship of bitterness to burnout, "Closely related to idealism and unfulfilled expectations is bitterness, the most significant factor in burnout" (p. 74). One source of bitterness is a lack of forgiveness toward oneself, fellow team members, national friends or even God for disappointed expectations. Our lists of past grievances against teammates can grow quite long! We may look back on how hard we have worked and feel our work was neither appreciated nor replicated by others on our team. Few of us work for recognition, but words of encouragement would go a long way in keeping us going. And yet, those words might never come. Whether it is due to poor team relationships, "sheep stealing" or rivalry in ministry, there seems to be no shortage of bitterness in the missions' community.

Certainly the staircase analogy shows the giving of oneself as a factor in burnout. Robynn worked hard preparing to get overseas; she diligently studied language; she learned to cook from scratch. She invested her life in her family and in her community. She gave through her health and in her sickness. She kept giving even as she went down further on the ladder. Idealism might suggest to us that if we can just give more and do more, things will change; or if only someone else on the team would work harder, we could accomplish our goals. The bitterness comes when things or people do not change. Both lead to the basement of burnout. Read one woman's struggle with never measuring up and imagine how easy it would be for bitterness to grow:

I have always struggled personally with never feeling like I measure up to my own expectations of myself, much less God's or other people's. So when people are unresponsive and your ministry seems fruitless, you don't always see what God is doing in the unseen world and it's easy to lose sight of the Truth and listen to Satan's lies. Also, it's not always big stresses of life, but just the composite weight of a thousand little things that are on your back that can get you down.

Sanford (1982) notes a number of difficulties facing clergy that can cause burnout. These include an unending job, lack of immediate and tangible results, repetition, constantly dealing with expectations, working with the same people (many of whom are needy) and failure. All of these are extremely relevant to missionary women. In America there is a saying that a woman's work is never done. There is always more laundry to do, dishes to clean, meals to cook, rooms to tidy. Add to this list of never-ending chores the unending tasks of crossing cultures, practicing hospitality, doing evangelism and discipleship and a missionary woman is hit hard with seemingly endless demands. Such demands may be even more extreme for women working in poverty-stricken areas or with refugees from war-torn areas. Missionaries often go overseas expecting immediate results, but after years of seeming fruitlessness, discouragement and bitterness can make their home in these women's hearts, making them more susceptible to burnout.

Dodds (1997) points out that the qualities needed for ministry are also qualities that open the door for burnout. "The values inherent in ministry are for self-giving, sacrifice, working for change in the self, others and the social context. In a sense, these are dangerous values, 'setting up' the opportunities for failure and burnout" (p. 1). It seems ironic that the very things that make a person want to go into ministry are the same things that may push that person toward burnout. It could be that one of the most important skills a missionary brings with her is that of knowing herself, her strengths and weaknesses, her gifts and abilities, her boundaries and personal limitations. The ability to say "no" is vital, as well as the discernment to choose to mainly work in areas of strength and gifting.

Missionary women need to seek the Lord for an accurate perspective on their expectations when those expectations don't match reality. Mission agencies also need to look at their expectations of their leaders and workers. In reading Robynn's story in chapter two, I must say that I felt compelled to look more closely at what we as mission leaders are asking capable leaders to do. If missionaries do a good job of handling responsibilities, we add more responsibilities to their ministry description. How much should leaders be expected to handle?

Almost all resources on burnout have inaccurate or unrealistic expectations as a common factor. Writers and counselors recognize a correlation between expectations and burnout. The question is, how strong is the link between the two? To what extent are expectations and burnout related? Most authors mention expectations as a cause of burnout and many believe they are a significant factor. Unrealistic expectations are often cited as main contributors to burnout by people in helping careers. Missionaries experience burnout more than people living in the United States, whether those people are in full-time ministry or lay people. Dyment (1989), who did his dissertation on "Burnout among missionaries: An empirical inquiry into the role of unrealistic expectations, job role ambiguity and job role conflict," asserts that it is apparent from literature that the "height of our expectations is an important factor in burnout" (p. 122). The research from Dyment's (1989) study correlates missionaries' unrealistic expectations with two of Maslach's three burnout factors: emotional exhaustion and personal accomplishment.

It is important to understand the difference between realistic and unrealistic expectations. One can work to reach attainable expectations; however one cannot meet those that are unreachable. To keep working at the impossible in one's own strength is a recipe for disaster. We know that God can do the impossible. But sometimes we try to be Him and forget we are not. We take over His role of trying to convict people of sin and save their souls. We grow discouraged when, after we share the gospel, our friends don't come to know Jesus. We try to change people's hearts and open their blind spiritual eyes when that is not our task. Only God saves. We proclaim the gospel. We pray. We trust. We give God our lives to use as He wills. When He doesn't do what we think is best on our timetable, we are faced with a choice: we must either trust Him or work harder and longer trying in vain to accomplish what only He can do.

Some evidence hints at male and female missionaries reporting the same levels of burnout; however, Dyment (1989) also mentions the need for more investigation into this issue. And, in fact, Chester's (1983) research documents missionary wives' tedium/burnout scores as higher than the missionary husbands' scores. He also reported counseling more missionary women than missionary men with symptoms of burnout.

According to my research, there is a significant and pervasive gap between expectations and reality among missionary women and I believe this gap indicates that expectations definitely have a role in burnout. Practically every expectation listed on the survey I conducted was unmet in a person's reality. Women didn't pray as much as they thought they should and weren't as fruitful, spiritual or strong as they thought they should be. In areas of ministry, team, personal practices and relationships, missionary women didn't measure up to who they thought they should be and didn't do what they thought they should do. As a result of this widespread discrepancy between expectations and reality, possibly along with other contributing factors, missionary women have had experience with not only some of the symptoms of burnout, but burnout itself.

Some missionary women reported that they had experienced burnout; others have felt close to it; and some were unsure whether or not they had experienced it. (Some of those surveyed declined to answer.) We've already mentioned that 80 percent of the missionary women surveyed felt close to burning out. I want to emphasize this: eight out of every 10 missionary women have felt close to burnout. Nineteen percent reported that they had in fact experienced burnout.

There was no distinguishable difference in the percentage of those who experienced burnout between married women and single women; similarly there was no significant difference in burnout occurrence between those who had children and those who did not. According to the survey there was no increase or decrease in burnout based on length of service. My biggest surprise came when the survey results showed that there was no difference in burnout among those who worked in creative access countries and those who didn't. For some reason I thought those who worked in creative access countries would have a higher rate of burnout.

An interesting finding is that single women had higher expectations than married women in 18 of the 34 areas. Their expectations weren't always significantly higher, but they were higher. Here is how the averages of expectations compared between those who were married and those who were single according to the survey:

Expectation	Singles	Married
1. Have a daily quiet time.	3.82	3.81
2. Have a best friend on her team.	2.56	2.31
3. Embrace her new host culture.	3.65	3.57
4. Be fruitful.	3.51	3.49
5. Be growing spiritually continually.	3.52	3.83
6. Have a successful family life.	3.44	3.61
7. Be a prayer warrior.	3.44	3.48
8. Enjoy national friendships.	3.48	3.36
9. Have a strong relationship with her supporters.	3.35	3.22
10. Stay connected with her sending church.	3.29	3.27
11. Be a good public speaker.	2.60	2.55
12. Teach well.	2.82	2.71
13. Be spiritually dynamic.	3.14	3.03
14. Be brave & unafraid of new circumstances or trials.	2.77	2.84
15. Have good leadership in her organization.	3.18	2.94
16. Have a strong team.	3.10	3.02
17. Continually trust God for everything.	3.70	3.73
18. Have a sure and certain calling to her work.	3.80	3.76
19. Persevere no matter what.	3.23	3.25
20. Have high standards for herself and her family.	3.32	3.44
21. Not experience burnout.	2.58	2.72
22. Be a strong leader.	2.51	2.56
23. Have miraculous stories to tell how God is using her.	2.56	2.73

24. Not fail.	2.59	2.60
25. Be admired by people for her calling.	2.54	2.42
26. Be well cared for by her organization.	3.35	3.15
27. Be accountable to leaders in their church and org.	3.52	3.52
28. Succeed in every area of life.	2.42	2.57
29. Be well balanced in areas of ministry in and out of home.	3.03	3.20
30. Be certain about her roles and able to do them all well.	3.07	3.03
31. Be content without a lot of money.	3.23	3.45
32. Sacrifice her happiness for her husband's ministry.	2.44	2.47
33. Be a trail blazer.	2.49	2.39
34. Feel confident in ministry.	3.19	3.06

However, though single women initially had higher expectations, married women had a wider gap between expectations and reality than single women on 27 out of 34 of the areas surveyed. Notice the average differences between expectations and reality in the chart below:

Expectation	Singles	Married
1. Have a daily quiet time.	-.58	-.69
2. Have a best friend on her team.	-.48	-.43
3. Embrace her new host culture.	-.48	-.57
4. Be fruitful.	-.98	-1.18
5. Be growing spiritually continually.	-.86	-1.04
6. Have a successful family life.	n/a	-.57
7. Be a prayer warrior.	-.95	-1.02
8. Enjoy national friendships.	-.36	-.56
9. Have a strong relationship with her supporters.	-.55	-.57
10. Stay connected with her sending church.	-.46	-.64
11. Be a good public speaker.	-.20	-.06
12. Teach well.	-.03	-.14
13. Be spiritually dynamic.	-.77	-.77

14. Be brave and unafraid of new circumstances or trials.	-.23	-.41
15. Have good leadership in her organization.	-.52	-.27
16. Have a strong team.	-.62	-.46
17. Continually trust God for everything.	-.75	-.76
18. Have a sure and certain calling to her work.	-.13	-.25
19. Persevere no matter what.	-.08	-.16
20. Have high standards for herself and her family.	-.18	-.12
21. Not experience burnout.	-.19	-.46
22. Be a strong leader.	-.01	-.28
23. Have miraculous stories to tell how God is using her.	-.61	-.89
24. Not fail.	-.52	-.56
25. Be admired by people for her calling.	-.34	-.26
26. Be well cared for by her organization.	-.11	-.10
27. Be accountable to leaders in their church and org.	-.14	-.40
28. Succeed in every area of life.	-.34	-.60
29. Be well balanced in areas of ministry in and out of home.	-.64	-.73
30. Be certain about her roles and able to do them all well.	-.35	-.54
31. Be content without a lot of money.	-.12	-.38
32. Sacrifice her happiness for her husband's ministry.	n/a	-.23
33. Be a trail blazer.	-.29	-.32
34. Feel confident in ministry.	-.38	-.46

So though singles had higher expectations in more areas, they only had seven areas where the difference between expectations and reality were higher than the married women's. These seven areas were (1) having a best friend on her team, (2) being a good public speaker, (3) having good leadership in her organization, (4) having a strong team, (5) having high standards for herself and her family, (6) being admired by people for her calling and (7) being well cared for by her organization. I wonder if these seven areas where single women feel more tension than married women are possibly due in part to married women having a husband who (1) can be a good friend on the team; (2) possibly speaks more in public than she does; and (3) is usually considered the leader in their relationship as he and she together follow the leadership of the organization. The single woman may (4) be more dependent on a team for relationships than a married woman; (5) have higher standards for herself without a spouse or partner to speak into her life about perfectionism; (6) be more admired because she goes out alone and often to places where finding a future spouse is less likely than in her home country; and (7) be more dependent on her organization to care for her, since she is on her own. It seems like a co-worker or a team could help in some of these areas, and I'm sure there are other factors of which I am unaware as a married missionary woman.

Whether married or single, no missionary woman is consistently meeting most of her expectations. The survey clearly shows that both married and single women missionaries are equally susceptible to burnout. Single missionaries might not have a partner to help monitor them closely regarding how they are handling expectations or how many hours they are putting into ministry. Single women can sometimes become too focused and, without feedback or help, may find themselves overcommitted quite easily in their ministry outside their homes, while trying to keep up with what they need to in their homes. Married women have things to do for another person, meals to cook, a house to clean or possibly children to care for in their home, as well as demands and a desire of ministry outside her home. At times missionary women may feel like giving up due to all they have to do. When asked what makes them feel like giving up, women who completed the survey responded:

ﾕ Overwork—trying to do three full-time jobs simultaneously without resources and experience. Doing something that I'm not really trained for, physical challenges (no electricity, no water, rats in the house), harassment from men in my community, endless meetings where I get bored and frustrated. Working with other staff who are very culturally different from me. Endless requests for money from friends and strangers.

So many different things hit at different times and in differing degrees. Having the cultural barrage of robberies, friends being discouraged by betrayal of nationals, government corruption, local corruption, horrid traffic all the time, fear of crime, the endless needs, feeling like my help is hardly even a drop in the bucket, kids struggling with school or friendships or self image, husband's stress with his job, coworkers or other factors. All these things play into feeling like quitting.

The never-ending awareness that I'm a failure as a missionary. Knowing that I'm a disappointment to a lot of people. My physical problems. Mind-sapping chronic fatigue. Feeling so apart from the rest of our missionary community, even though I love them very much. Tired of hearing languages I don't understand; it would be nice to be able to have a normal conversation with strangers, instead of the dread and embarrassment that comes because my language abilities are so poor. Tired of trying to come up with decent meals; not wanting to spend the money it would take to prepare better meals, even if I wanted to cook, which I don't anymore. Tired of living in our current house, because of its location. Tired of being asked how many people I've witnessed to this month. I'm tired of hanging on and not giving up in the face of long, difficult trials. I'm tired of living far away from our children. Once they went to boarding school, they were gone, and they're still gone. I'm really tired of giving up my children. My father is in poor health, and my mother in better health, but still aging quickly. Even though I have family around to give them excellent attention and care, still, I'm tired of not being there. My father is probably going to die before we can retire in two years. It's hard. It's stressful being an older missionary in an increasingly young missionary force, not that we don't love and appreciate the much younger ones, but it gives you the feeling of being passé; of being a dinosaur.

Reading their stories brings tears to my eyes. Women who left with high expectations desiring to serve the Lord are facing and surviving unbelievable challenges to honor Him. Of course they grow tired and may even feel like giving up. However, they don't have to burn out. Though I am sure there are other causes of burnout, we can conclude this chapter recognizing that there is a correlation between expectations and burnout among missionary women. There are also other contributing factors to it, some avoidable (such as having no boundaries, unattainable expectations and perfectionism) and others that are inevitable (hardships, family background and culture stress).

There are two important things to do in response to the information in this chapter. First, missionary women need to be aware of the symptoms and causes of burnout. Second, they need to develop a personal plan to continue on in ministry while proactively working to avoid burnout. The next chapter gives some practical help in dealing with this one factor in burnout: expectations.

Survival Tip #10
Count your mosquito bites

In July 1996, I (Robynn) attended a seminar on Black Islam presented superbly by Dr Carl Ellis. I'll never forget one of the illustrations he used to describe the effects of accumulated racial injustice. He said racism was like a mosquito bite. If you only get one in any given day it's no big deal. Some one makes an unfortunate comment. You brush it off as ignorance, you scratch the bite a little, but as you ignore it, the itch subsides. It's fine. However if you get 47 mosquito bites a day—a racially insensitive joke, an unfair generalization, a look, a direct encounter, a "flesh color" crayon that doesn't match your skin tone— you are miserable. The itch becomes unbearable. You can't ignore it. And if you wake up to a new day and 47 more bites, it's all you'll think about. You become obsessed. Your skin screams out for relief. You are inflamed and raw. It's hard to think of anything else.

It was a vivid illustration then and I think it also works now to help explain one of the causes of burn out. If only one thing happens to you, if you only get one mosquito bite—if you only experience chronic dysentery for an extended amount of time— most likely you will not burn out. You can scratch that one little bite a little, but eventually you'll be ok. You'll move on. But if like in Dr Ellis' illustration, you get 47 mosquito bites a day, it's more than you can endure, especially if the same mosquitoes bite you every single day, for several years in a row. Burn out can be the result of that build up of lots of things over time.

I've already listed many of my mosquito bites—death of a friend, staph infection, persistent spiritual warfare, madmen on our roof, death of a neighbor's child, another friend's infertility, another friend's miscarriage, a new believer turns back, too many responsibilities, sickness, death of our landlord's son. Any one of these things, had it happened in isolation, would not have put us over the edge. It was the accumulated effect. We got too many mosquito bites, over too many days, and weeks, and months and years. No amount of antihistamine would reduce the itch. We scratched ourselves raw.

It might help to take some time to identify your mosquito bites. What are the things that are "itching" you? How many bites are you getting a day? How are you coping with this? Is there a remedy for the pain? Is it time to get away from these pesky insects for a spell? Take some time to make your list and to pray through it. Show it to your leadership. Get some advice. Gain perspective.

ELEVEN

EXPLORING SOLUTIONS, DEALING WITH EXPECTATIONS TO AVOID BURNOUT

Self-exploration and self-understanding are the cornerstones of self-renewal and are an antidote for burnout and excessive life stress. – Dennis T. Jaffe

Because there is such a strong correlation between expectations and burnout, addressing and adjusting this one area—expectations—in the lives of missionary women has the potential to increase fruitful, long-term service. When realistic, faith-filled missionary women are aware of what their expectations are, and what they might encounter in service, they are braced for reality. At the same time they look to God, who is at work doing the impossible in His own good time and in His own ways, even through and in the midst of difficulties and heartache.

Though we've looked at missionary women's expectations of God, the church, host culture and teammates, we are going to focus in-depth on just two parties that have responsibilities in this area of resolving and aligning expectations. Missionaries themselves and the mission agencies that send them both have a role to play in adjusting and clarifying expectations so that burnout can be avoided.

As missionary women give up their unrealistic, idealistic expectations for themselves (Dodds, 1997; Taylor, 1997; Jones, 1995; Rediger, 1982; Perry, 1982; Melendez, 1983; Jaffe, 1984), they may see God use them to change the world. When missionary women set realistic goals for their ministries and learn to say no to others' ideas for them (Jones, 1995; Minirth, 1990; Perry, 1982; Melendez, 1983; Kotesky, n.d.), they may get to know themselves, their limits, gifting and energy levels better. Self-knowledge is vital. Jaffe (1984) supports this when he writes, "Self-exploration and self-understanding are the cornerstones of self-renewal and are an antidote for burnout and excessive life stress" (p. 128). Such knowledge and understanding helps missionary women recognize and work within their own limitations and boundaries. Some of us are low-energy people and others are high-energy.

We cannot compare ourselves with each other. We look to God for guidance in how to invest the energy we do have, and we recognize that He has made us all differently. Praise God for the high energy people who are able to work and work and get a lot done. Praise God for the low energy people who work and work to get a lot done. We work at different speeds and in different amounts, but we all are able to be faithful to God

The parable of the stewards encourages us in a similar way. To some He might have given a lot of energy (ten talents), to others some (five talents) and to some not a lot (one talent). The steward with one talent was berated because he didn't invest his talent, not because he didn't make as much as the man steward with ten talents. We can all invest the energy He has given us to the best of our ability. Jesus doesn't compare the value of our time and energy, but does hold us accountable to be faithful with what he has given us. We can ask God to use us to do the impossible, but we cannot demand that He do it in our way or according to our time table, or even that he do it at all. Working harder will not ensure the miraculous. Giving all that we have still cannot meet everyone's needs. We have to leave room for God to be God

... leave space for the unanswered prayer. Purposes we may never know about or understand may be at work—purposes we may thwart if we overextend ourselves to try to "fix" a situation.

We cannot and should not judge others for what they are or are not accomplishing as they prayerfully set their goals and seek to be faithful to God's call on their lives. One of the most hurtful statements to me that I read in this research is that missionary women are often the most critical of other missionary women. How sad! We may judge because we feel bad about ourselves—a judgmental attitude makes us feel we aren't so bad after all because other women are also "bad" in our judgment. Is it possible we judge because we set some goals that involve the assistance of others, who have not set goals to be a part of our plans? Or, we may have chosen to adopt some unrealistic goals and resent those who are not similarly pushing themselves. So, we who are judging need to examine our own heart to determine what is behind our judgment of them.

Also, we ought to offer our co-workers understanding rather than judgment: consider the issues of educational decisions, energy levels, personality of the children, personality and gifting of a woman, her marital status, her husband's contribution or lack thereof, age and season in life, health, financial support and her faithfulness in tasks of which we are unaware. Rather than criticizing, we have the opportunity to be loving, helping, listening to and encouraging each other. Yes, we may lovingly confront when it is necessary, but always with gentleness and a view to help. We each trust God to work in and through us and our teammates. His power is perfected in our weakness. We look to Him for guidance, not comparing ourselves to other people or them to us, as we develop our ministry plans and trust Him to be at work.

Future missionaries also have expectations. Potential missionary women going on a short-term mission trip before deciding to be a career missionary may develop expectations that are more realistic and gain a more balanced picture of what life and ministry might look like (Smith, 2004; Eitel, 2008). Such a trip gives them a chance to interact with missionaries and watch them in their "habitat." The example of these missionaries living day by day and sharing honestly about their struggles will go along way in helping these potential missionaries have insight in making decisions about their future. They may discover sooner that God will do more in them than through them (Love, 2000,) and may recognize God's desire to work in his children and the importance He places on character development. These women may begin to see missions, not simply as God working in others, but as a wonderful opportunity for God to delve into their lives to shape them into the image of Jesus Christ.

Before going overseas I did not think I had an anger problem. I thought I had a close walk with God. I thought my husband and I had a solid marriage. I thought I had my act together. Living in another environment showed me that I had growing to do. There is nothing like living in a different culture to bring out areas in our lives that God needs to work on so that we can continue to be used by Him effectively. He works in us so that He can work through us. Though the difficulties faced may be painful, missionaries who persevere will grow more spiritually and ultimately be more effective in their ministry.

Missionary women who know themselves, their personality, weaknesses and limits, and who also get regular exercise, rest and enjoy vacations (Minirth, 1990; Perry, 1982; Blaine, 2001; Melendez, 1983; Foyle 2001; Dodds, 1997; Kotesky, n.d.) may enjoy a longer career in missions. Missionaries need more than a vacation; they should go on a pilgrimage (Sanford 1982). Vacations can be empty and are differentiated from pilgrimages by their different purpose: "A pilgrimage also is time away from the regular routine, but it involves a journey or sojourn for a planned and sacred purpose" (p. 28). Johnny Miller, former president of CIU talked at length at a Christar conference about rest and renewal. One of the things he's identified as a good vacation is not retreating from life but retreating to Jesus. Having a day of rest is critical as well. Miller also once wrote in the Christar publication, *Heart to Heart,* that sometimes taking a nap is the godly thing to do:

> One of the most spiritual things Christian workers can do sometimes is take a nap. It's good not only for you, but for everyone who has to work with you.
>
> Excessive stress damages the body, leading to such things as coronary heart disease, cancer, lung ailments, accidental injuries, cirrhosis of the liver, suicide. It plays a role in MS, diabetes, genital herpes, and trench mouth. The same germs attack everyone, but over-stressed people succumb more.
>
> But it also damages relationships. The shoe string that snaps on the way to church, the dead battery in traffic, the broken dish when company is coming. It's the unrelenting accumulation of little things that rob us of peace, of control, of rest.
>
> In my U.S. culture some of the best-selling drugs, like Tagamet and Pepcid, treat the symptoms of stress. That's interesting because we live on an island in time which enjoys the highest standard of living in history, with much leisure time; spawning industries that sell us multiplied options on how to spend our leisure. Yet with all this "leisure," we have more stress-related illnesses. Why? Because in our leisure we've not learned to rest.
>
> There's no slowing down, no withdrawal, no recovery, no rebuilding. We leap into leisure at the same pace we worked. But leisure and rest are different. We need to understand the principle of the Sabbath before our ignorance chases us into a premature grave. I say "principle" of the Sabbath. I am not a

"Sabbatarian," bound to Moses' law. But I think that the Law is a wonderful guide when used lawfully.

"Sabbath" is an untranslated Hebrew word. It does not mean "seven," but "stop, cease, rest." It referred weekly to one day in seven, and annually to three set feasts: Yom Kippur (Lev. 16:31), Trumpets (Lev. 23:24) and Booths (23:39). There was even a year designated for rest, Jubilees (Lev. 25:8). These were festivals, fun family times, but also rest time, devoted to the Lord.

Because the Sabbaths were devoted to the Lord, they were to be holy, different from the ordinary, special to the Lord. This included putting aside all ordinary labor (except acts of mercy or life-saving necessity). And it included all laborers, who on the Lord's Day became God's free people, all equal before God. These cessations were not merely withdrawal from work, but withdrawal to God.

There is always more to do than there is time for. When we rest, we will actually have the emotional and physical energy to do what must be done.

In some agencies it is difficult to get missionaries to take their vacations! Money is usually tight; there is nowhere to go. When children are little there is really no such thing as a vacation for the parents. It is just doing what you normally do in a different place! However, what a delightful difference a change of scenery and a break from the norm can bring! It is worth the extra hassle and headache to take that vacation, even if it is just exchanging houses with a friend across town! It is important for missionary women to recognize their need to get away from the strain that they live with. Sometimes single women will get together with friends and take a vacation together. Not only is it more cost effective, it is fun to have friends on a vacation and there is accountability to actually get away for a while. There are several retreats like "Single

Vision" (http://singlevisioninternational.com) that are specifically geared for single missionaries as well.

Missionary women should consider setting aside a yearly time of planning and evaluation as a helpful time to reflect on values, use of time, ministry and goals over the past year as well as planning for the coming year. Such a time might include one of the available burnout inventories during their time of self-evaluation and goal planning (Rediger, 1982; Perry, 1982). While women don't need to be paranoid and constantly fret about burnout, taking one day or one weekend each year for thoughtful self-examination and planning, as well as making any necessary changes as a result of the evaluation, may help prevent burnout and encourage a long and fruitful ministry.

Another way to adjust expectations and avoid burnout is to cultivate relationships with people who are able speak into our lives (Jaffe, 1984; O'Donnell, 1992; Koteskey, n.d.). Missionary women can seek to develop a support group of people who care and who hold them accountable and who may help them maintain good health wherever they live. These people could include a network of supporters from the home church, national friends, missionaries from other organizations or our own teammates. I remember that at a particularly stressful time for me and my husband, our teammates gave us a weekend away at a nearby hotel. They took turns watching our four children (what a wonderful and brave team!) so that we could rest and be together. We were blessed. We were not offended by their offer to help. We were thankful. We need teammates and need to seek to be teammates who are proactive and not just reactive. How much easier it is to help others prevent burnout than it is to help them recuperate from it.

Mission agencies also have a responsibility to be sensible, realistic and helpful to missionary women so they can have long-term careers and avoid burnout. From the beginning, agencies have the opportunity to educate and train missionaries about expectations and burnout (Taylor, 1997; Dyment, 1989). When candidates come with high expectations, we must gently educate them on the rigors of missionary life. I remember visiting with a missionary family in a south Asian country who, in their first term, had been robbed more than once, moved with their two small children several times in a short period of time, had electricity sporadically and fought off illness as well as a vicious attack of bees.

I was sitting at their table and asked them how they did it. How were they enduring such opposition? I will never forget this young man's response, "It is a high calling." Though they went through many struggles, they had been well prepared. Mission leaders can help missionaries think more about this high calling involving sacrifice, and less about their high expectations of all they are going to accomplish.

As my husband and I were planning a move back overseas, leaving our children and grandchildren, I was counting the cost and thinking it was a very high price for me to pay. At about that same time we were listening to several missionaries share about their previous term's experiences. I was overwhelmed by the sorrows being expressed, the challenges being faced and the heartaches that they shared. My heart cried out to God, "It is too much, Lord. The price is too high to pay." The Holy Spirit gently reminded me that though the price was high, Jesus is worthy. I pondered that the higher the price you pay for something, the more evident it is how worthy and valuable it is to you. And my heart cries of "it is too much" turned into a time of worship as I focused on the worthiness of Jesus. As mission agencies train new workers, a theology of suffering needs to be a major theme: counting the cost and following the Lord for His glory among the nations.

On their first home assignment, Robynn recognized that she and Lowell had not been adequately trained in suffering. They had been trained in church planting, in language acquisition, in team dynamics, in conflict resolution, but they had not been trained in suffering. All through Scripture we see that suffering is the place of growth for the Christian. As we participate in the sufferings of Christ (Col 1:24) we experience an intimacy with Him that we don't necessarily experience during seasons of joy. Paul wrote that he was willing to endure all things for the sake of the elect, that they might come to faith in Christ (2 Tim 2:10). He was willing to suffer anything. In countless places we read of endurance and perseverance. What do we endure? We endure suffering and the resulting sorrow. We do not endure alone, though. We are strengthened "with all His glorious power" (Col 1: 11) to endure. God is so committed to our endurance that He strengthens us for it! We need to prepare ourselves to suffer and suffer well, for the sake of the unbeliever and for the glory of God.

Another aspect of training is getting missionary women ready for what God might accomplish in them before He does more through them. In order to join a mission, people must fill out an application, have references and recommendations by their home church, communicate their statement of faith, have ministry experience, feel called and pass a battery of personality and biblical knowledge tests. They usually come to a mission agency fairly mature in their faith and fairly confident of who they are as believers in Jesus Christ. When they arrive overseas, it can come as a complete surprise to them that they have so many areas of need where God wants to work in them to conform to the image of His Son. Missionaries need to be prepared to go into cross-cultural ministry as ready learners, not merely of a new language and culture, but of God and His Word.

Much of the training that mission agencies give to their members is general and not gender-specific. It is true that there is much in training for missions where gender is not a determining factor, but there are some things that should be addressed in training for women. Mission organizations must help women be prepared for their multi-faceted roles in the home and outside of the home by presenting true pictures of life and ministry by experienced missionaries. They must give training about expectations in those different roles and how unrealistic expectations can lead to burnout. Some mission agencies provide training on cooking from scratch, dealing with sexual harassment, home schooling, security guidelines and balancing roles. Providing women with tools and resources to pursue their walks with God is also important. Having experienced missionary women train other women in evangelism and discipleship is critical. The ways women evangelize are often very different from the methods men use to evangelize, at least in the Muslim world.

For a conference on equipping missionary women, mission leaders were asked what the weaknesses were in training missionary women. One leader felt there is a definite lack in addressing woman-specific concerns similar to those mentioned in the previous paragraph during orientation and training. Not only was the lack of training mentioned, but also the lack of an agency-wide support for women during their first term. That is, women were not provided all that was needed to ensure their adequate language and cultural acquisition.

Another area which was felt to be deficient is that of training missionary women in their spiritual life. It is of supreme importance in missions that women be able to feed themselves spiritually and be responsible for their own spiritual growth. I'm not sure if it is because she is expected to already be capable in this area, or if it is assumed she will grow and develop on her own, but more and more mission leaders see the need for input and training for missionary women in their identity in Christ and their understanding of grace. Too often a woman's sense of worth is tied up in what she does, not in who she is in Christ. This can lead to a performance-based valuation of her own worth and that of others.

It isn't just the women's spiritual life and discernment that needs to be developed, but also her foundation for emotional wholeness and well-being. When a missionary woman is facing challenges, illness and discouragement, she will need as many resources as possible. Books and seminars are not sufficient; she benefits from competent counselors when needed. Such help would also be valuable in facilitating good team relationships and establishing trust with others.

One other area that was mentioned as deficient in training women missionaries is that of preparing them to set realistic expectations and goals. To me, this reinforces the importance of a book like this, which addresses some of these expectations and goals. More important than a book, though, is mission agencies being more intentional in helping women think through their expectations and goals. Regular interviews where direct questions are asked about missionaries' goals, their discouragements and challenges will give the mission insight into the needs and emotional health of women members.

Leaders in missions should take a good look at these areas and begin adjusting their training programs to address some of these key needs women missionaries have. The better equipped the missionary, the more realistic her expectations. The more realistic her expectations are, the better her chances for avoiding burnout and ministering long term. Does this mean agencies will have some separate training sessions for men and women? Perhaps; but perhaps men need to be educated about these areas as well, in order to better understand and serve their female co-workers.

By testing newcomers' personality types and values, agencies can see how missionary women handle stress and ascertain if they might be more liable for burnout due to their particular set of personality traits (Foyle, 2001). A tendency toward perfectionism, a history of sibling rivalry and poor family relationships in their family of origin can all be factors in burnout. Knowing the results of personality tests can help in country and team placement. As mission agencies are careful in making assignments and placing people, taking into account missionaries' age, gifting, personality and training (Dodds, 1997), they may sustain and retain missionaries with less burnout and more long-term fruitfulness. A helpful resource organization for mission agencies is Clarion Consulting (https://www.clarionconsulting.com). They specialize in helping teams by providing testing and discussion that helps each team member know their best contribution, as well as how they can most effectively work together as a team.

Mission leaders can also help women develop a clear, correct ministry description so that missionary women know the parameters of their job. This gives the women a framework from which to work as they pray about and explore where to invest their time. Freedom and accountability can be built into these ministry descriptions. Having clear guidelines helps women set boundaries, understand their roles and determine how best to invest their time. Having a wise and understanding leader go over these descriptions with her can help erase doubts and fears about her contributions to the ministry. In this way, missionary women and their leaders can more clearly understand one another regarding roles and expectations.

Mission agencies can also regularly evaluate their leaders, their training and standards. Through this evaluation, they may be able to determine if they are keeping up with trends, understanding the younger work force and training new missionaries appropriately (O'Donnell, 1992). There are ongoing seminars and instruction for mission agencies in these areas that must be utilized. Agencies should also be evaluating how they advertise mission opportunities and how they might be contributing to unrealistic expectations of newcomers. Assessing what is produced through their media and adapting it accordingly will also help prepare the next generation of cross-cultural ministers.

With the caution that mission leaders need to be sensitive to the needs and concerns of those in middle management of missions, I would encourage mission agencies to utilize mentors. Expectations need to be clarified for mentors and mentorees, but as mentors are intentionally orienting and doing all that can be done to ensure new missionaries' health and fruitfulness, missionaries have a greater opportunity for a full career of effective ministry. Having experienced missionary women come alongside those who are newer is critical.

I remember, and several other missionary women mentioned on the survey, how it was when we first went overseas. Mission agencies sent leaders to visit us in order to encourage and help us in our ministry. In the beginning only a man would come. He might spend hours interacting with the missionary husband. They would talk strategy and trends, make plans and set goals. He would have an appointment with the missionary wife at a certain time and possibly spend thirty minutes asking questions and listening to her. We appreciated them, but what a difference it made when missions began sending couples to visit. Women felt more heard, more valued and benefitted immensely from the mentoring they received from missionary women with vast experience. Missionary women had the opportunity to ask questions and have them answered. We could bring up our fears more openly and receive reassurance from someone who truly understood our situation.

Men and women minister differently and their circumstances are not the same. In our area of the world men would discuss theological issues and debate ideals in coffee shops or outings. Women shared their lives and questions over tea and cooking lessons in homes. Women need women mentors who know what it is like to minister to women across cultures. Mentoring certainly had an effect on one of the women who filled out the survey:

> I am very fortunate that I served cross-culturally for 2 ½ years before I got married and had children. When I was on the field as a single woman, I had a lot of neat married women around me and I learned a lot from them about what it was like to be on the field married. So I think that my expectations

coming back to the field married and with children were pretty accurate.

Other women share examples of experiencing mentoring from a distance and how that mentoring helped them be prepared for missions. They discuss how their own expectations were adjusted and shaped by others and their realness in sharing their lives. They also try to be open and honest about themselves, their joys and struggles so that they can help prepare the next generation of missionaries as well:

🌀 I'm thankful that Internet, Facebook, blogs and other outlets provide cross-cultural workers today with opportunities to show that we are living our lives in the same way that our supporters in the States do—we love the Lord, we serve Him, we care for our families, we fight with our husbands, we yell at our kids, we do stupid things, we fail the Lord, we repent, we pray, we weep, we struggle, we daily work out our salvation, we are daily being sanctified, we are daily dependent on the Lord.

🌀 I saw missionaries as highly devoted and motivated. They were realistic about the difficulties of being overseas, but showed joy in what God has invited them to do. I had developed friendships with some short-term missionaries and had a few that had many years experience. I also took missions classes in seminary as well as being involved in missions education with children in my church. I learned a lot from talking to the missionaries, reading books and studying the literature I taught to the children.

♫ During college, seminary and training, though, I think we were given a pretty realistic picture of workers and life on the field. We met a lot of workers who were really real. They opened themselves and their lives up to us. We saw normal people who were obediently following a calling that was not always easy but brought great joy.

As missionaries and mission agencies take responsibility and work to know, communicate and adjust missionary expectations, burnout may be more easily avoided as this one factor contributing to burnout becomes less of a threat. Missionaries can adjust expectations while still maintaining faith in God, who continues to do the impossible in and through His people around the world.

Survival Tip #11
Pray for maximum blessing even when you have minimum energy

Tina Henry, a dear co-worker of mine (Sue) for many years is a low-energy woman who serves the Lord with a big heart. She has learned a lot about serving the Lord with the energy she does have and writes about her experience:

The Minimum Woman is the title of the book that I have been saying for many years that I intend to write someday. Being an easy-going middle child with low blood sugar, and thus low energy, I have always felt that I have done a "minimum" job in all the roles I find myself having to balance as I seek to follow my Lord. Right now in the middle of my forties, I find myself wearing many hats, and sometimes feeling overwhelmed by them all. I pray daily for God to help me balance my responsibilities as a child of His, a wife, a mother of three, a Christian worker, a homemaker, a leader's wife, a neighbor, a Jr. high Bible teacher, administrator and board chairman of our kid's school, and a person with my own needs and desires! Help! No wonder I feel like I only have time and energy to do a minimal job in all these areas!

Admittedly, I have often handled the stresses of these responsibilities wrongly, trying to do them in my own strength. And over the years, I have suffered from various stress-related conditions including chest pains and a spastic colon. I praise God for good doctors, and medications that have eased my pain, but I have also been seeking from the Lord some ways to respond better to the stresses in my life. I discovered five principles that have been helping me deal with these stresses.

The first principle deals with priorities. When I was younger, I always felt that if I just worked harder, faster, and smarter, I could do it *all*. I could take on any new commitment that came my way with God's strength. Now as I am older, and have even less energy than before, I realize that I can't do it all. God ever intended for me to. I see now that I must be careful to do the most important things first, because I'll never get to all the good things there are to do. I must leave the undone things in God's hands, praying about those things, but realizing that I cannot do them all myself. If I waste time doing unimportant things, I will not have the priority things finished when my time and energy runs out. This entails saying "no" to many things.

The second principle involves people. Since there are things that need to be done and I can't do it all, I am learning that it is good to get others involved and to have them do some of the things I can't do. I can have my husband and children help some around the house, or hire a maid to do the cleaning. I can pray for God to bring someone else to take over children's church, knowing that we are a body where everyone works together using their gifts to do the Lord's work. We must work in partnership with others.

The third and fourth principles to keep in mind are patience and persistence. Some things take a long time to accomplish, like learning a language or developing meaningful friendships. We need to persevere, knowing that these things will not be accomplished in a day. It is good to break such long-range goals into pieces and pray through each one, looking to God to bless our efforts one step at a time.

Finally, the last principle is that of multiplication. Back when I was involved in a college ministry group, our leader spoke to us on this principle from the story of the boy with five loaves and two fishes. We were trying to raise money as a group to fly to a national discipleship conference. He brought out that we needed to do all that we could to earn the needed cash, but then we needed to trust God to multiply our small efforts, just as He multiplied the boy's small lunch to meet the needs of many thousands. So our group went door-to-door offering our services to clean houses, baby-sit, and whatever we could. We earned a fair amount, but nothing close to our need. But somehow God multiplied our efforts and we were all able to attend the conference. Every day now, I pray that God will multiply my feeble efforts in each area of responsibility to meet the needs of others. I look to Him to see what He wants me to be involved in, and as I do all I can in each area, minimal though it might be, I can expect Him to multiply my efforts to the blessing of others. I would find life very overwhelming if I didn't know we serve a powerful and gracious God at work. This relieves a lot of pressure, for He can maximize our minimal efforts for His glory and the blessing of others.

You may have noticed that prayer has been mentioned in each of the principles above. It is the most important ingredient of all in our relationship and work for the Lord. It over-rides and envelopes all else. It is by prayer, that we know what our priorities should be; it is through prayer that we can ask God to send people to do the jobs that we cannot do ourselves. Prayer helps us to keep God's perspective on things, thus enabling us to have patience and perseverance. Asking God to multiply our small resources, we can see great blessing come to others.

TWELVE

ROBYNN'S CONTINUING STORY AND SOME OF OUR CONCLUSIONS

Two and a half years later, I can say I'm not the same frail person that boarded that plane leaving South Asia with two bewildered little girls. Time has passed and with its passage, a certain degree of healing has occurred. I would love to claim that I'm as good as new. I would love to say that I've bounced back to who I used to be. Neither of those two things is true; but it is true that God has been at work in my heart soothing, healing, comforting and restoring. It's been a slow climb out of despair and although I certainly haven't yet reached the top, I have gained ground. I have reached a higher place where the air is clearer and thinner. God is good.

I probably should have written this chapter first when I felt healthier, stronger. Writing out the stories in this book, particularly the ways God disappointed me in chapter eight, wreaked havoc on my soul. Once again I experienced the bitter pains of heartache. What reads as words, nouns and verbs, actually were environmental devastations to the landscape of my soul. It's been extremely difficult to live it again. I've cried over this keyboard. I've sobbed as the words flowed out onto the page. And I've wondered if I'm "better" enough to write a chapter 12 after having endured again chapters two, six and eight, not to mention all the other stories hidden in Sue's chapters.

As I've relived the burnout and as I've read through Sue's material, I've felt a keen pressure to write the rest of the story with honesty and authenticity. This chapter has to be real or Sue and I are guilty of over-simplifying. If we're not honest with you, we are merely noisy gongs. If you are hurting, a glib remark in the face of your pain, a trite comfort is salt in the wound, vinegar in the scrape. Those things hurt deeply. The original wound hurts almost worse in the face of the pat answer, the Romans 8:28 thrown at your soreness.

Sue and I want to offer you hope. If you're just starting out into the adventures of missions, we want realism and the grace of Christ to temper your expectations. If you've burned out somewhere along the way, we want you to remember there is healing, there is strength for tomorrow. Burnout is not the end of your story.

Not long after we returned from India, I remember mumbling to Lowell, wondering if I'd ever be the same again. His response was interesting. He said we wouldn't want to be the way we were. The years in India have shaped us. God used each story to disciple us in profound ways. We learned lessons about His glory, about His mercy, about His holiness. We came to understand more of the mysteries of God. We know by experience that He literally provides water in the desert, that He really is our Shade at our right hand, that His joy actually gives us strength. We are different. These lessons are ours "for keeps." We wouldn't want to be unchanged. We wouldn't want to be the same again! Heaven forbid! And I've come to think that Lowell is right. The broken Lowell and Robynn have resulted in a transformed Lowell and Robynn. Our theology has been remolded. Our understanding of who He is and who we are is refitted. The things we take on, the things we stew over, the people we feel responsible for, those things have all been remodeled.

After packing up and leaving our home for all those years, the girls and I flew south to some dear friends where we stayed for one week. I was still physically recovering from staph infection, severe amoebic dysentery and 18 days of antibiotics, let alone the heat, packing, goodbye parties and a thousand last minute errands and details. Spiritually I was battered and beaten down. Emotionally I was ruined.

Our friends, Wilson and Kamala, were the perfect people to collapse with. They took such gentle care of the girls and me. Auntie Kamala played games, held tea parties, provided crafts and crayons. I took long naps. Wilson fixed hundreds of cups of tea. I sat in a chair in the middle of their sitting room and pathetically cried through nine complete Gaither Homecoming DVDs. In the past I'd made fun of that music—the hairspray, the makeup, the dramatic, the crescendo; now it was the balm that soothed. Kamala fixed delicious meals to tempt my appetite again. Their adult children, Sharon and Gaius came to visit. There was lots of laughter, lots of love and lots of space to begin to heal.

Lowell and Connor returned from their hiking exploration of the Himalayan Mountains and our family was reunited in the capital city. Together we flew back to North America, stopping first at my parents' place in Ontario for more sleeping, more rest, more delectable meals, some walks, a few outings, the beginnings of a few conversations. These things were all good and necessary. We needed to recover physically. We were absolutely spent, exhausted and finished.

Our sending agency hosts a week of debriefing for those back from the field. Mandatory attendance made us a little grumpy to begin with, but it was such an important first step. There we heard fellow survivors' stories. There we were able to share our stories. The deep level of connection with other furloughing workers was a comfort and provided a sense of community in what felt like a lonely journey.

Two significant conversations stand out in my mind from that week. Debby, a long-time friend from the past, having heard our stories of Amy Jo's death, Shivraj's death, George Uncle's death among all the other stories we shared, remarked on the level of grief we had experienced. She hugged us both and told us that it would take a long time to get over it all. There was too much grief.

The second conversation involved Sue and her husband Don. In a quiet office interview where we felt the freedom to share some of the ways the mission had disappointed us and wronged us, Don and Sue heard us and it visibly grieved them. They apologized sincerely on behalf of the organization.

Two months after moving out of our ancient stone home along the great Ganges River where the mango tree dominated our courtyard, surrounded by temples, mosques and a million people, we arrived in Kansas. The contrast couldn't have been greater. Where we had known noise and bustle and crowds, we now had to adjust to quiet prairies, a systemic busyness and individuals living isolated lives. Where we had experienced endless purifying rituals we now were faced with an obsession with bacteria-free cleanliness. We had been the master of a three-ring circus, the juggler with all his balls and bottles in the air, the center of the tire with spokes of activity stemming from our house—at least that's how it felt. Now suddenly, with all of that activity stopped, there was an unnatural quiet. Lowell and I went through withdrawal. In South Asia my phone would ring 20 times or more a day. In Kansas I found myself opening my phone, pushing buttons, holding it to my ear just to make sure it was still working! I repeatedly heard phantom knocks on the door and would run, kicking into hospitality mode on the way, only to discover the wind was teasing me; no one was there. Having been programmed to intuitively understand that the housewife's spirituality is judged by the cleanliness of her house in South Asia, I cleaned our house trailer in Kansas with a vengeance: the first three weeks I scrubbed our kitchen floor every day!

Our sending church welcomed us warmly and with great love. Our house was ready. They had cleaned and furnished it for us down to the sheets on the beds and groceries in the cupboards. It was amazing. We were loved on. People were sensitive to our needs, wanting us to have the space we needed, but also wanting to invite us into community. Our church family opened up their arms to the battered sent ones with mercy and tenderness. They didn't think of us as failures. They seemed to respect us for our vulnerable confessions. We weren't doing well and they provided the care we needed.

A friend who had known us in Asia told me that I would need to learn how to do nothing. I remember nodding at her and thinking, "how on earth does someone do nothing? ... " Days later with tears streaming down my face, I called her on the phone and asked her how. How does a person do nothing? I needed lessons. My insides were still spinning. How did I stop? Sweetly, she simply instructed me to go to my couch, to sit down and to look out the window. That was it; that's what doing nothing looked like.

The mission had urged us to not schedule any meetings during the first three months. We needed to take time to process our Indian lives. Things needed to settle. We needed to gain some perspective. That was good advice. By the time October rolled around it felt like we might be ready to report back to our sending church what God had done. We shared the stage with our dear friends and partners in ministry, Donnie and Beth, who were also on home assignment at the time. Together the four of us recounted the ways God had been at work in the church plant, in the lives of believers, in the lives of unbelievers, in our leadership, in our teams. Telling it all out loud, sitting there with people who really knew what all had happened behind every photo, knowing the details Donnie and Beth weren't sharing, remembering how the lights had been off during that event or how we'd had no water for three days during that crisis ... these unspoken details together with the photos in our Power Point presentation swung me back into a dark place. It was too early to remove the bandages from my hurt. Doing so only uncovered what had been concealed. The wound was still raw and messy. I entered a type of depression afterward that was hard for me to articulate, hard to categorize. I felt empty, lonely, fatigued and sick to my stomach, full of dread, with a heavy weight over me.

At the end of November my grandmother died. I flew to Northern British Columbia to attend her funeral. It was a special time together with extended family. Cousins who had been children were now adults. Aunts and uncles had suddenly grown old and were now grandparents themselves. We were able to honor Grandma and the influence she had had on each one of us as she had spurred us all on to faith and good deeds, obedience and sacrifice and hard work.

The morning that my dad and I were each scheduled to return home after the funeral, we gathered for breakfast at Grandpa's house with the few still left in town. Auntie Carol was there from South Carolina, Uncle Henry from Ontario and, of course, Grandpa, Mom and Dad and I. Auntie Carol served up the hot cream of wheat cereal and Grandpa asked Uncle Henry to pray. There are certain prayer rules in Grandpa and Grandma's house. While Grandma might have been more flexible on these things, Grandpa certainly wasn't. When you are asked to pray for a meal, you pray for the meal. You might ask that God "bless this food to our bodies use;" you further might ask that God bless those that had prepared the food; but you didn't stray from matters regarding the meal itself, or the cooks of said meal.

When Uncle Henry began to pray, he forgot the prayer rules of the house. He started in on an elaborate prayer for, of all things, Robynn and Lowell. He prayed for our blessing, for the children, for their success in school, for their transition to this new country. He prayed for rest for our bodies, recovery for our souls. He prayed for healing and restoration. He asked God to strengthen us to do His will.

While he was praying I began to wiggle in my seat. I was embarrassed by the prayer. Didn't Uncle Henry remember he was only to pray for the cream of wheat? Didn't he understand that

Grandpa's porridge was getting cold and there's nothing Grandpa hates worse than cold porridge? However when the prayer was over and we all looked up, I realized that everyone else had entered into that prayer. They all were wiping tears from their faces. They had all been agreeing with Uncle Henry. When God heard Henry's prayer, He heard all of those dear relatives' prayers. I was the only one that had been thinking of the porridge.

Returning to Kansas I had a new energy. The dark clouds had parted. The depression's worst was over. God had given me the space I needed to walk out into healing. It was a tangible change in reality. I felt it. It was a much needed step toward restoration.

In the middle of our family's transition and newly begun recovery, the prospect of more change was introduced. Not long in to the New Year, my husband Lowell began to sense God leading us in a completely new direction. I should have seen it coming. Lowell had dropped clues. God Himself had begun to nudge my spirit in a new direction, but by continuing to pursue a return to India, I thought I was being loyal to our calling, to the people we had left behind and to God himself, really.

As the reality of a change in direction took hold in my heart, a deep panic set in. Lowell, who has always been a visionary thinker and planner, was full of the possibilities. His mind never stopped dreaming of what God might do in this new adventure, how this might affect global missions and the opportunity to reach the least-reached. He was passionate and excited, full of dreams and new ideas. God was giving him a new calling and I was freaking out. As I responded to Lowell, trying to help him think reasonably about some of these new plans (or at least that's what I thought I was doing), Lowell was hurt by my lack of support, my critical attitude, my rejection. I, in turn, couldn't understand why he couldn't understand what I was saying. Our communication became barbed and ugly. Every time I tried to talk to him, I hurt him. Every time he tried to articulate something to me, he hurt me. Painfully. Deeply. We fought for several weeks. Nothing was ever resolved. It was a horrible season. I wanted out. Weighing my options, it seemed that the least damaging one was for me to leave for a time and let Lowell have some space. Communicating that seemed to be the slap in the face we both needed. We realized we needed help desperately.

Lowell picked up the phone and called Ken and Diann, a couple in our sending church who counsel hurting people through a combination of wise advise, prayer and listening to God. Through our season of counseling with them, I came to understand at a deep heart level three profound, world-view changing truths.

First of all, I began to grasp that God really does love me. He notices me. He sees me. This is the type of lesson you learn in Sunday school. This is the prerequisite to growth in Christ, yet somehow I'd skipped it. I didn't connect with that love. I had preached it to others but I didn't believe it to be true of me. I didn't realize how He's not really that impressed with what I do, especially the stuff He hasn't asked me to do ... but He is impressed with me! He treasures me! He loves me! He created me and of all creation I am his prized possession (Isaiah 43:1; 62:5, James 1:18).

Secondly, I realized that my pain matters to God. He doesn't overlook me. I had always believed that my pain is insignificant compared to others who have deeper hurts, whose pain is paralyzing, who are debilitated by their wounds. I've had it in my head that God looks at all the hurting people and he says, "Come on Robynn, let's help them out." I'll never forget the sensation when my counselor explained that if there are two or three people wounded in a car accident, the paramedics don't overlook the person who was hit by a motorcycle to save the two hit by the truck. Each person is given the care they need. My pain was not insignificant. It mattered that I was hurting. God saw it and He cared! He called out to me, "Come on, Robynn, come over to me. You're hurting. Let me love you. Let me comfort you."

The third truth I learned is that I am not responsible for other people and their emotional, physical and spiritual needs, or their pain. Early on I began to believe that it was my job to make everybody okay. I was the one that had to fix the tension in the air. I had to make people happy. I was the one that had to figure out what was wrong and make it better. I had to apologize, even if I wasn't sure the offense was mine. Somehow I was responsible that I wasn't able to take care of everyone. I was letting them down. That thought devastated me. I processed our decision not to return to India, which was very threatening for me. Inside I bore the weight that I couldn't possibly disappoint our team and the wider community, our friends there, our church, our sending agency. During the counseling slowly, gradually, haltingly I began to hear God speak into my soul. He reiterated that He alone is responsible. I don't have to take care of everyone. I could hand other people and their needs and pain over to Him. He would be in charge. He would take care of people. If they were disappointed, ultimately they were disappointed in Him. I was off the hook.

You can imagine how these three lessons, unlearned over the years of ministry, would significantly contribute to my burnout. They were directly linked to my expectations of myself and God. If I believed, and I did, that God's love for me was tenuous and fragile, then it made sense that I'd work unrealistically hard to be lovable and to win his favor. If I really believed, and I did, that my pain didn't matter, then it made sense that I would ignore the tremendous sorrow and grief in my soul and my exhaustion; it made sense that I would ignore my own desperate need for care, roll up my sleeves and continue to serve the more obviously hurting around me. If I further believed, and yes, I truly did, that I was solely responsible for others around me and for their health, happiness and success, then it made sense that I would sacrifice myself at any cost to take responsibility for these things. I would bear their disappointment. I would take it personally. I would try to keep them happy. I would monitor their faces and see the rippling of failure and displeasure and it would sit like a dead weight in my stomach. I would physically sense in my chest the tightening, the building anxiety. When I walked into a room, I always was aware of who I had disappointed and that I could never fully make it right. My expectations of myself were confused with my expectations of God and of others.

God, the Great Teacher, planned my fall semester to include a field trip back to South Asia. Months before our counseling began, months before these lessons surfaced, I was asked to lead a group of women back to the city where we had served on a short-term mission trip. At the time when I was asked, I was excited by the opportunity to return for what I thought would be a mid-furlough visit. However when the dates approached for our trip, it became apparent that God wanted to use the trip to emphasize the lessons He'd been teaching me. He had it in mind that I would be the one to go back and tell our community, our team, our South Asian friends that we would not be returning. The thing I most feared, disappointing them all, was what God was asking me to do, yet with the newfound realization that it wasn't actually me at all that was disappointing them. What an unbearably difficult assignment this was. I was petrified to see the faces of our dear friends when I told them. The fear paralyzed me. Lowell and Ken, our counselor, scripted my lines for me. They helped me outline what I would say, the actual words.

Those two weeks back in South Asia with those amazingly brave women from our sending church were some of the most difficult weeks of my life. I faced my deepest heart fears and issues, admitting to people that I was disappointed in God's leading, but that it remained true that God was leading us away from Asia. The emotional stamina it took to warmly greet people in one breath and then bid them farewell in the next breath seemed unprecedented to me. Those four women prayed me through those difficult days. They wept with me even when they didn't understand the depth of my confused emotions.

Good friends and teammates Donnie and Beth, who had returned to South Asia and were eagerly expecting us to return, had expectations of long ministry careers side by side with our family. They were also walking through their own disappointment with God. In their own grief they sustained me during mine. God asked me to say goodbye to our lives, our calling, our teammates, our friends, our community and, in a strange way, to my childhood and to huge parts of my personality (which, truthfully, lie dormant and irrelevant while outside of Asia). I did it and it didn't destroy me, although it felt like it might.

That trip was a year ago. Now, as I am writing, Lowell is there with my parents collecting our stuff. They've sorted and waded through years of accumulated bits and pieces, toys, pots and pans, saris, bangles, letters, files. I can't even imagine how hard that's been. As Lowell said on the phone the other night, "this job would have killed you, Robynn." And he's right.

And so it's pretty final. God is asking us to stay on here in North America for the sake of the new thing He's called us to. We will obey. Obedience is better than sacrifice. I can't understand all the paradoxes at work in my soul. As difficult as the years in Asia were, I find myself longing to return, yet I'm relieved to not go back. I miss the daily sufferings—the constant push into who God is. I was desperate for God there, even in the daily mundane details. Water coming from the tap wasn't guaranteed. I needed God to supply. And how often He did. Miraculously. Lavishly. And yet I've come to love the ease of living here—the comforts and the luxuries, the availability of goods and the promise of water in the tap. Where do these paradoxes come from? How should I best process them?

I still experience many of the residual burnout symptoms. I would have expected to be well by now, but if we've learned anything in this book, it's that our expectations are rarely to be trusted. So I've tried to lay those out before God and let Him lead the way to healing. Many of my fuses are still blown. Where

I used to serve up meals and teas to countless guests with a laid-back flair for hospitality, I now find myself nervous and worried to invite people in here in North America. I'm not sure how it all works. I'm not sure what the cultural rules are for hospitality and it makes me stressed to think about it too much. Only recently have I thought, "We should invite the Jones over," and it's been a happy prospect! I think I can do it now and enjoy it.

New things still are ridiculously daunting. After two years I've learned how to go to parent-teacher conferences at the elementary school. Now our son is in middle school. His first conference was a very scary thing for me. It was different and I wasn't sure how to do it. As silly as it sounds, my palms were sweaty; I was nervous and on edge anticipating the event as well as attending it. Such a small thing doesn't merit such an extreme response, but I've come to see that this is the long, slow part of recovery. I still battle anxiety and waves of unexplainable fatigue. I still get really tired really quickly. Sue says it takes a long time. I've settled into that "long time" idea and it's okay; I'll be all right eventually.

I still wonder at the strangeness of God. My parents are exploring an overseas calling again in South Asia. How strange is that? Why would God lead them there now, after we've left? If the work force is low, why on earth would God lead us away? We know how to live overseas. Why would He ask us not to? That seems strange to me.

I'm still getting better. I'm working through the fear of Lowell's visions. Previously these have worn me out, because I thought that in order to not disappoint him I'd have to rise to the occasion and put those ideas in place. But now I know God is sovereign over those visions. The ones He's ordained will come to be even without me. I'm responding better to each idea. I'm not threatened by them. I've come to see how God has uniquely gifted Lowell, and I celebrate that.

I struggle with deep loneliness. It's the elephant in the room of my soul. It's always there. Our closest friends remain in South Asia. Over the years we formed intense friendships as we suffered together, worked together, prayed together. It's not easy to make such friends. I'm learning that and I'm trying to ignore that elephant and reach out to people here, even though that represents another new thing and makes me afraid. God has given me developing friendships ... and I'm learning to be patient. These things take time.

Reading back through this book, I've realized again that Sue and I don't have all the answers. We've come to see, through research and experience, that faulty expectations set the missionary woman up for disappointment. We've discovered that if not adequately processed, over time, these faulty and unmet expectations set her up for burnout. It's a pattern Sue has seen repeatedly and I've lived.

I wish I had done things differently during my time in South Asia. I wish I had learned that my teammates were human, that they would disappoint. I wish I had clarified and known our home church's expectations of us. That simple conversation might have saved me from a lot of guilt over the years. I wish I hadn't gotten so uptight about South Asia and her expectations of me. I wish I hadn't thought that I was God and that I would rescue dying Hindus, save my neighbors and rescue my teammates. I really wish I wouldn't have tried. It undid me. I wish I would have known that God loves me, and it doesn't matter what I do or where I live, that love doesn't change. Knowing God's love for me, knowing that He treasures me, would have made His sovereignty less maddening, I think. I wish I would have known that.

While we don't have all the answers, there are a couple of things that we should remember. Let us never forget we are engaged in a battle. Our enemy is not our roommate, our spouse or our children, our sending agency, our teammates, our sending church, our local neighbors or even ourselves. Although it may feel at times like we battle it out in the trenches against these opposing forces, these are not our enemies. Our real enemy is the enemy of our souls, the father of lies, Satan. He prowls around roaring and we feel the hot air of his breath and his spittle on our faces as he tries to destroy us and others. He uses deception (*Robynn, you mustn't disappoint . . . Robynn, this is your responsibility*) and he specializes in wearing us down. He'll speak lies into our souls while all the while messing with our circumstances. Lowell and I have come to call those intense spiritual blitzes as "the realm of the ridiculous." You know it when it happens. Last night both of the headlights in our car went out. Mystified I stepped out of the car only to lose one of the lenses from my eyeglasses. Coming in to the house I discovered the kitchen sink had backed up! That was the realm of the ridiculous. Remember to call Satan's bluff. Remind him that you belong to and are loved by the Most High God. He has no place in your lives or in your circumstances.

Please also remember that burnout is not failure. Burnout is merely another tool God uses to mold us and transform us further into the likeness of His son Jesus. Burnout represents another form of suffering. Scripture is full of references to suffering. Suffering is our privilege. As we participate in (enter into, take a turn at) the sufferings of Christ, we also enter into that redemption process. Paul spoke of being willing to endure all things that the elect might come to faith. Enduring burnout is a part of that.

We die to our own expectations. We let them go. We release them to our heavenly Father who is good and who knows all things. We bask in His Sovereignty and His control. The Christian faith is all about death and rebirth. There is a cycle of grief and hope, death and life, surrender and joy, burnout and restoration. Burnout puts us in the place to be broken and to submit to our own humanity. We realize we are not God. We further realize that *God* is God. He's in charge of our growth, our spiritual development, our journey. Burnout is just one spot on our growth chart. We go on to be used by God again, in a new and healthier way, in a way that reflects our limitations and our deeper dependence on God.

Take the time to quickly forgive those that have wronged you or disappointed you because they didn't meet your expectations. Along the path there are ample opportunities for us to choose forgiveness and peace, or bitterness and the destruction of our souls. Forgiveness keeps our faith supple and strong. Holding onto grievances weighs us down, prematurely ages us and can even cause physical health problems. Christ urges us to forgive. He set the ultimate example of forgiveness when, even on the cross, He chose to forgive those that brought about His death. Forgive your local friends, forgive your teammates, forgive your leadership, forgive yourself, forgive God.

Remember also the worthiness of the Pearl of Great Price. One day Lowell took one of the pearls from a necklace of mine. He dropped that pearl in a beggar's bowl in the heart of the city. At a team meeting later that afternoon he spoke about the Pearl of Great Price. When he was finished elaborating on Scripture, he told the team that there really was a pearl hidden in the city. It was out there, ours for the finding. In the parable the man loves the Pearl so much he is willing to sacrifice all things to acquire it. This has become a precious theme to me. There are things I love about my passport country: hot running water, tortilla chips, cheese whiz, coffee crisp chocolate bars, Tim Horton's donuts—and yet I love the Pearl more, much more. There's no comparison. I will sacrifice anything to acquire it. Writing this now, it strikes me that this willingness to sacrifice has to persist. There are things I love about Asia. Will I sacrifice those to acquire the Pearl of Great Price who is here, patiently waiting for me to start looking? The Pearl is worthy.

South Asia aged me. I'm 39 years old in a 49-year-old soul. Living overseas for 14 years has changed my perspective on life, on the poor, on the disproportionate distribution of wealth, on the environment and politics, on tribulations and heaven and death. I gave my youth and naiveté to the Great Commission. I traded them for the privilege of suffering in the place of greater growth. I gave them up for the sake of the few that God had chosen in our riverside town. And I survived! I survived the Great Commission. I lived through my own expectations and devastations.

By God's sweet and kind grace, the cross of Christ did not crush me. God called me to it and then He alone brought me through. Burnout is not my destination; it's not who I am or who I've become. God is still transforming me and using me. Admittedly I don't see it as clearly. Right now it looks remarkably different. It's quieter. I get to do more things for Him backstage. Maybe He likes it better this way, because now I *know* its all about Him. I have learned the hard way that I can't do it anymore. If it's going to happen, it's going to have to be Him making it happen. He gets all the credit and all the glory now and *that* is as it should be.

*   *   *   *   *   *   *   *

In the middle of writing this book I (Sue) half jokingly asked the question, "Can a person experience burnout from writing a book on burnout?" At times the writing, rewriting and more rewriting felt overwhelming and I wanted to quit. I was tired, cranky and felt like I was failing. None of those feelings were comfortable. At other times I was excited, inspired and loved the writing process. That was more fun. There were times when I walked away from it to take a much-needed break and other times when I knew I had to persevere and keep writing. By God's grace I kept the end goal in mind, remembering back to the hard labor and amazing delivery of my four children and how the hard work was well worth it in the end, and I endured. The book is done.

Writing a book and serving cross-culturally must be similar. There are times when both are overwhelming in their scope, awesome in how God provides what is needed, mundane in dealing with details that just need to be taken care of. Breaks and vacation days are needed as well as those times when we just have to grit our teeth and keep at it. Communication is vital as we work together toward a common goal. In writing, Robynn and I grew in our appreciation of each other and worked through some differences. We listened to each other and worked not just to complete the task, but to build our relationship. We took constructive criticism and made changes; we laughed and we cried as we worked through chapter after chapter. We knew we wanted to work together, we knew what we wanted to do, and we challenged, encouraged and inspired each other along the way. We were a team.

Robynn and I have wanted to honor God through the writing of this book. Our insights and stories, the research and input from the women who serve cross-culturally around the world hopefully all came together in a way that will help all of us who are burdened by the lost in this world to be more fruitful and effective for the glory of God.

It is our prayer that as a result of this book God would help missionary women to recognize any unrealistic expectations they have of themselves and to align their expectations, braced for reality, while walking by faith in God. We hope that mission agencies will be better equipped to send out well-prepared missionaries through training, care and clear communication. May God continue to bless churches and establish deep ties with those they send out in missions to touch the world. We trust that teams will work hard together, love each other and live as members of His body, letting God use the display of His power in community to transform societies where they live.

May we all burn bright, not burn out, for Him as we use our resources wisely, walk closely with Him and praise Him for His work in us and through us for His glory.

Oh God, give grace to the weary, hope to the brokenhearted, peace to the stressed, joy to the disappointed and endurance to us all. Amen.

APPENDIX A

SAMPLE SURVEY

Dear Co-Worker,

I have been doing some research on the relationship between expectations and burnout. I have read what the experts say and would like to do a short survey to see what people have experienced. I would deeply appreciate your help by taking the time to answer the questions below so that we can gain a better understanding about the possible gap between expectations and reality and if that might contribute to burnout. It might take about 15-20 minutes to complete this survey.

This survey has three sections. The first section deals with what you think are the expectations of women as cross-cultural workers. There is a list of qualities and/or actions where you put a designated number based on what you think is expected from cross-cultural workers. The second section consists of seven questions where you write in your answers. You can be as thorough or as succinct as you would like. The more details you include, the better for me. Probably the less time you spend, the easier it is for you! Thank you for doing what you can. The last section has the same list of qualities and/or actions as the first section, but this time you put in the number that designates *your* perception of how *you* live out your daily life.

Please complete the survey and email it back to me as an attachment. If you want to remain completely anonymous, feel free to fill it out, print it and mail it to me so that I get it by

April 30: Sue Eenigenburg, my mailing address. You could use the same for the return address. If you don't mind letting me see your results (which I will compile immediately for research, not pour over individually and will keep confidential) then just email it back to me as a completed survey. Whichever you would like to do is fine with me. I will gladly send you the results of this study and what the ramifications might be for cross-cultural workers, our agencies and cross-cultural work in general.

Thank you,
Sue Eenigenburg

BEFORE YOU BEGIN:

What is your home country? _____

What organization are you with? _____

How long have you been involved in cross-cultural work?

_____

Are you in a creative access country? ____ (yes) ____ (no)

Are you married? _____ (yes) _____ (no)

If you have children, how many do you have and what are their ages? ____ (0-5) ____ (5-10) ____ (10-15)____ (15-19)_____

As a cross-cultural worker, have you ever felt close to experiencing burnout? _____ (yes) _____ (no)

As a cross-cultural worker, do you think you've experienced burnout? _____

SURVEY FOR WOMEN WORKING CROSS-CULTURALLY
Please insert number in the blank that most closely aligns with your opinion:

1 – rarely   2 – sometimes   3 – often   4 – always

<u>Expectations</u> for women working cross-culturally are that she <u>should</u>:

1. Have a daily quiet time. _____
2. Have a best friend on her team. _____
3. Embrace her new host culture. _____
4. Be fruitful. _____
5. Be growing spiritually continually. _____
6. Have a successful family life. _____
7. Be a prayer warrior. _____
8. Enjoy national friendships. _____
9. Have a strong relationship with her supporters. _____
10. Stay connected with her sending fellowship. _____
11. Be a good public speaker. _____
12. Teach well. _____
13. Be spiritually dynamic. _____
14. Be brave and unafraid of new circumstances or trials. _____
15. Have good leadership in her organization. _____
16. Have a strong team. _____
17. Continually trust God for everything. _____
18. Have a sure and certain calling to her work. _____
19. Persevere no matter what. _____
20. Have high standards for herself and her family. _____
21. Not experience burnout. _____
22. Be a strong leader. _____
23. Have miraculous stories to tell of how God is using her. _____
24. Not fail. _____
25. Be admired by people for her calling. _____

26. Be well cared for by her organization. _____
27. Be accountable to leaders in their fellowship
    and organization. _____
28. Succeed in every area of life. _____
29. Be well balanced in areas of service in and out of home._____
30. Be certain about her roles and able to do
    them all well. _____
31. Be content without a lot of money. _____
32. Sacrifice her happiness for her husband's service/work._____
33. Be a trail blazer. _____
34. Feel confident in service. _____

*   *   *   *   *   *   *   *

1. How is your role as a cross-cultural worker different from what you expected?

2. What do you think your sending fellowship expects from you?

3. How has your organization not met your expectations?

4. How did you view cross-cultural workers before you became one and how did you develop this image of what they would be like?

5. What has surprised you about team life and working with other cross-cultural workers?

6. What symptoms of burnout do you think you have experienced? (i.e. difficulty in sleeping; weight loss; lack of interest in food; headaches and gastro-intestinal disturbances; a chronic tiredness; depression; boredom; other)

7. What stresses are you experiencing that make you tired and feel like giving up?

1 – rarely   2 – sometimes   3 – often   4 – always   N/A
if not applicable

Being <u>real and honest</u>, in practice I:

1. Have a daily quiet time.   _____
2. Have a best friend on my team.   _____
3. Embrace my new host culture.   _____
4. Am fruitful.   _____
5. Am growing spiritually continually.   _____
6. Have a successful family life.   _____
7. Am a prayer warrior.   _____
8. Enjoy national friendships.   _____
9. Have a strong relationship with my supporters.   _____
10. Stay connected with my sending fellowship.   _____
11. Am a good public speaker.   _____
12. Teach well.   _____
13. Am spiritually dynamic.   _____
14. Am brave and unafraid of new circumstances or trials. _____
15. Have good leadership in my organization.   _____
16. Have a strong team.   _____
17. Continually trust God for everything.   _____
18. Have a sure and certain calling to my work.   _____
19. Persevere no matter what.   _____
20. Have high standards for myself and my family.   _____
21. Do not experience burnout.   _____
22. Am a strong leader.   _____
23. Have miraculous stories to tell of how God is using me._____
24. Do not fail.   _____
25. Am admired by people for my calling.   _____
26. Am well cared for by my organization.   _____
27. Am accountable to leaders in my
    fellowship and organization.   _____
28. Succeed in every area of life.   _____

29. Am well balanced in areas of service in and out of home. _____
30. Am certain about my roles and able to do them all well. _____
31. Am content without a lot of money. _____
32. Sacrifice my happiness for my husband's service/work. _____
33. Am a trail blazer. _____
34. Feel confident in service. _____

BIBLIOGRAPHY

Beck, J.A. (1992). *Dorothy Carey, The tragic and untold story of Mrs. William Carey.* Grand Rapids, MI: Baker.

Blaine, A. (2001). *Before you quit.* Grand Rapids, MI: Kregel.

Chester, M. (1983). Stress on missionary families living in "other culture" situations. *Journal of Psychology and Christianity, 2*(4), 30-37.

Crawford, N., & Devries, H. M. (2005). Relationship between role perception and well-being in married female missionaries. *Journal of Psychology and Theology, 33*(3), 187-197. Retrieved April 15, 2008, from PsycINFO database.

Dodds, L. A., & Dodds, L. E. (1997). *Am I still me? Changing the core self to fit a new cultural context.* Retrieved June 03, 2008, from Heartstream Resources: http://www.heartstreamresources.org/membcare.htm

Dodds, L. A., & Dodds, L. E. (1997). *Stressed from core to cosmos: Issues and needs arising from cross-cultural ministry.* Retrieved June 03, 2008, from Heartstream Resources: http://www.heartstreamresources.org/membcare.htm

Dodds, L. A., & Dodds, L. E. (2000). *Love and survival: Personality, stress symptoms and stressors in cross-cultural life.* Retrieved June 03, 2008, from Heartstream Resources: http://www.heartstreamresources.org/membcare.htm

Dyment, W.E., (1989). *Burnout among missionaries: An empirical inquiry into the role of unrealistic expectations, job role ambiguity and job role conflict.* Unpublished doctoral dissertation, Rosemead School of Psychology, Biola University, La Mirada, CA.

Eitel, K. E., ed. (2008). *Missions in Contexts of Violence.* Pasadena, CA: William Carey Library.

Elmer, D. (2006). *Cross-Cultural Servanthood.* Downers Grove, IL: InterVarsity

Foyle, M. (1986, July). Burnout or brownout? *Evangelical Missions Quarterly.* Retrieved October 23, 2007, from the Gospel Communications Web site: https://bgc.gospelcom.net/emqonline/emq_article_readpv.php?Article ID=3228

Foyle, M. (2001). *Honourably wounded.* Grand Rapids MI: Monarch.

Golden, J., Piedmont, R. L., Ciarrocchi, J. W., & Rodgerson, T. (2004). Spirituality and burnout: An incremental validity study. *Journal of Psychology and Theology, 32*(2), 115-125. Retrieved April 15, 2008, from PsycINFO database.

Hall, E. M., & Duvall, N. S. (2003). Married women in missions: The effects of cross-cultural and self gender-role expectations on well-being, stress and self-esteem. *Journal of Psychology and Theology, 31*(4), 303-314. Retrieved April 17, 2008, from PsycINFO database.

Hawkins, K. (1994). Missionary "super moms". *Journal of Applied Missiology, October.* Retrieved April 26, 2006, from Halbert Institute for Missions: http:www.bible.acu.edu/missions/page.asp?ID=451.

Irvine, J., Armentrout, D. P., & Miner, L. A. (2006). Traumatic stress in missionary population: Dimensions and impact. *Journal of Psychology and Theology, 34*(4), 327-336. Retrieved April 15, 2008, from PsycINFO database.

Jaffe, D. T., & Scott, C. D. (1984). *From burnout to balance.* New York: McGraw-Hill.

Jones, M. (1985). *Psychology of missionary adjustment.* Springfield MO: Logion.

Koteskey, R.L. (n.d.) *What cross-cultural workers ought to know about burnout.* Retrieved June 03, 2008, from Cross Cultural Workers Web site: www.crossculturalworkers.com

Maslach, C., Schaufeli, W. B., & Leiter, M. P. (2001). Job burnout. *Annual Review Psychology, 52,* 397-422. Retrieved April 15, 2008, from Academic Search Complete database.

Melendez, W., & Deguzman, R. M. (1983). *Burnout: The new academic disease.* Washington DC: Clearinghouse for Higher Education.

Minirth, F., Hawkins, D., Meier, P., & Thurman, C. (1990). *Before burnout.* Chicago: Moody Press.

O'Donnell, K. O. (Ed.). (1992). *Missionary care.* Pasadena CA: William Carey Library.

Perry, C., Jr. (1982). *Why Christians burnout.* Nashville, TN: Thomas Nelson.

Rediger, L. G. (1982). *Coping with clergy burnout.* Valley Forge, PA: Judson.

Sanford, J. (1982). *Ministry burnout.* New York: Paulist.

Schubert, E. (1993). *What missionaries need to know about burnout and depression.* New Castle IN: Olive Branch.

Seymour, J. (1995). *Time healing overcoming the perils of ministry.* Valley Forge, PA: Judson Press.

Smith, Ma. (2004). *Through her eyes.* Waynesboro, GA: Authentic Media.

Smith, Me. (2007). *Burnout: Signs, symptoms and prevention.* Retrieved October 19, 2007, from Help Guide Web site: www.helpguide. org/mental/burnout_signs_symptoms.htm

Swenson, R. A. (1992). *Margin.* Colorado Springs, CO: NavPress.

Taylor, William D. (Ed.) (1997). *Too valuable to lose.* Pasadena: William Carey Library.

Tomic, W., Tomic, D., & Evers, W. J. (2004). A question of burnout among reformed church ministers in the Netherlands. *Mental Health, Religion and Culture, 7*(3), 225-247. Retrieved June 03, 2008, from PsycINFO database.

Vander Pol, H. M. (1994). *Missionary selection, stress and functioning: A review of the literature.* Doctoral research paper presented to Rosemead School of Psychology Biola University, La Mirada CA.

Willard, D.. (2002). *Renovation of the heart.* New Press, Colorado Springs CO.

Zalaquett, C.P., &Wood, R.J. (1997). *Evaluating stress: A book of resources.* Lanham: The Scarecrow Press. Retrieved from Rutgers New Brunswick/Piscatawy Campus: www.rci.rutgers.edu/-jacksox/PDF/EvaluatingStress.pdf